PROMISE AND PERIL

BOSTON UNIVERSITY STUDIES IN
PHILOSOPHY AND RELIGION
General Editor: Leroy S. Rouner

Other Titles in this Series:

Promise and Peril

The Paradox of Religion as Resource and Threat

Edited by

Anna Lännström

UNIVERSITY OF NOTRE DAME PRESS

Notre Dame, Indiana

Library of Congress Cataloging-in-Publication Data

Promise and peril : the paradox of religion as resource and threat /
edited by Anna Lännström.
        p.   cm. — (Boston University studies in philosophy and
religion ; vol. 24)
        Includes bibliographical references and indexes.
        ISBN 0-268-03825-2 (cloth : alk. paper)
        1. Religion.   2. Violence—Religious aspects.
I. Lännström, Anna.   II. Series.

BL50 .P65   2003
291.1'78—dc21   2002151563

To Huston Smith
Philosopher, Religious Practitioner, and Wise Soul

His brilliant writings on world religions address our fear of the unknown, showing that other religions and peoples are not as dangerous and strange as they might seem and that all religions (ours and theirs) contain both promise and peril.

Contents

Preface

Boston University Studies in Philosophy and Religion is a joint project of the Boston University Institute for Philosophy and Religion and the University of Notre Dame Press. The essays in each annual volume are edited from the previous year's lecture program and invited papers of the Boston University Institute. The director of the Institute, who is also the general editor of these Studies, chooses a theme and invites participants to lecture at Boston University in the course of the academic year. The editor of each volume selects and edits the essays to be included in the volume. In preparation is volume 25, *The Stranger's Religion: Fascination and Fear.*

The Boston University Institute for Philosophy and Religion was begun informally in 1970 under the leadership of Professor Peter Bertocci of the Department of Philosophy, with the cooperation of Dean Walter Muelder of the School of Theology, Professor James Purvis, chair of the Department of Religion, and Professor Marx Wartofsky, chair of the Department of Philosophy. Professor Bertocci was concerned to institutionalize one of the most creative features of Boston personalism, its interdisciplinary approach to fundamental issues of human life. When Professor Leroy S. Rouner became director in 1975, and the Institute became a formal part of the Boston University Graduate School, every effort was made to continue that vision of an ecumenical and interdisciplinary forum.

Within the university the Institute is committed to open interchange on fundamental issues in philosophy and religious study which transcend the narrow specializations of academic curricula. We seek to counter those trends in higher education which emphasize technical expertise in a "multi-versity" and gradually transform undergraduate liberal arts education into preprofessional training.

Our programs are open to the general public and are often broadcast on WBUR-FM, Boston University's National Public Radio station. Outside the university we seek to recover the public tradition of philosophical discourse which was a lively part of American intellectual life in the early years of the twentieth century before the professionalization of both philosophy and religious reflection made these two disciplines virtually unavailable even to an educated public. We note, for example, that much of William James's work was presented originally as public lectures, and we are grateful to James's present-day successors for the significant public papers which we have been honored to publish. This commitment to a public tradition in American intellectual life has important stylistic implications. At a time when too much academic writing is incomprehensible, or irrelevant, or both, our goal is to present readable essays by acknowledged authorities on critical human issues.

Acknowledgments

First and foremost, this series would not be possible without the authors. They have provided us with thoughtful and interesting essays, for which they have received only modest compensation. In addition, their cheerful acceptance of editorial changes and strict deadlines has made the editing process easy and enjoyable.

I owe a great deal to Lee Rouner for his editorial help and for his enthusiastic and indefatigable support and to Barbara Darling-Smith for her attention to detail and her meticulous copy editing. Most of all, however, I am grateful to both of them for being such delightful colleagues! I also owe many thanks to Rebecca Schmidt for her help in running the lecture series that formed the basis for this volume, to Emily Lyman and Alison Downton for their assistance in preparing the manuscript, and to Adam Wright of Wheaton College for his hard work and competence in once again creating the author index.

As usual, Barbara Hanrahan, Jeffrey Gainey, Rebecca DeBoer, Wendy McMillen, and the rest of the staff at the University of Notre Dame Press have been a joy to work with! We continue to be grateful for their confidence in the Institute's work and their professional expertise in publishing this series.

Finally, we are grateful to the PEW Charitable Trust, the Institute for Religion and World Affairs, the Stratford Foundation, and the Boston University Graduate School of Arts and Sciences for their financial support of our lecture series on Promise and Peril from which these essays came.

Contributors

KAREN ARMSTRONG holds the B.A. and M.Litt. degrees from Oxford University and is now a full-time writer and broadcaster. Her television work includes "The First Christian," a six-part documentary on Saint Paul which she wrote and presented (1984) and two interview series, "Varieties of Religious Experience" (1984) and "Tongues of Fire" (1985). A prolific author on a wide variety of religious subjects, she has written *Muhammed: A Biography of the Prophet* (1991), *A History of God* (1993), *In the Beginning, A New Interpretation of Genesis* (1996), *The Battle for God* (2000), *Islam: A Short History* (2000), and *Buddha* (2001).

WENDY DONIGER earned two doctorates, one in Sanskrit from Harvard University and one in Indian Studies from Oxford. She is the Mircea Eliade Professor of the History of Religions at the University of Chicago. Her books include *The Ganges* (for children); *Siva: The Erotic Ascent* (which has been translated into French and Italian); *Women, Androgynes, and Other Mythical Beasts*; *Dreams, Illusion, and Other Realities*; and many others. She has lectured widely in this country and abroad, and is both a Fellow of the American Academy of Arts and Sciences and past president of the American Academy of Religion.

MARC GOPIN is currently Visiting Associate Professor of International Diplomacy and Senior Research Associate at the Fletcher School of Tufts University. His work focuses on the relationships among world religions, violence, and peacemaking, especially in regard to the Arab/Israeli conflict. He teaches a course on "World Religions: Violence and Conflict Resolution" and is the author of a paper entitled "This War Is About Religion, and Cannot Be Won Without It." He is the author of *Between Eden and Armageddon*.

ANNA LÄNNSTRÖM is Assistant Director of the Institute for Philosophy and Religion and Instructor in the Department of Philosophy, at Boston University. Her B.A. is from the State University of New York at Potsdam (*summa cum laude*). She has held a Presidential Fellowship at Boston University and received her M.A. in 1999 with a thesis in Indian Philosophy on the role of myth and metaphor in Advaita Vedanta. Her Ph.D. thesis argues that Aristotle's ethics is a viable option for contemporary ethical theory. Her work in progress is tentatively titled *Loving the Fine: Virtue and Happiness in Aristotle's* Ethics.

GERALD JAMES LARSON has taught and written extensively on comparative philosophy and religion in southern Asia. He is currently the Rabindranath Tagore Professor of Indian Cultures and Civilizations and Director of the India Studies Program, Indiana University at Bloomington, after more than twenty-five years as Professor of Religious Studies at the University of California, Santa Barbara. He is a past President of the Society for Asian and Comparative Philosophy. Among his books are *Interpreting across Boundaries: New Essays in Comparative Philosophy* (edited with Eliot Deutsch) and *Sāmkhya: A Dualist Tradition in Indian Philosophy.*

BHIKHU PAREKH earned his Ph.D. from the London School of Economics and is now Centennial Professor there. For many years he was Deputy Chair of the British Commission for Racial Equality. He was also Vice Chancellor of the University of Baroda, India, from 1981 to 1984. His books include *Hannah Arendt and the Search for a New Political Philosophy, Karl Marx's Theory of Ideology, Gandhi's Political Philosophy,* and (as editor) *Bentham's Political Thought.* He was elected the British Asian of the year in 1992, was given the BBC's Special Lifetime Achievement Award in 1999, and was appointed to the House of Lords in 2000.

IAN JOHN READER is currently Professor of Religious Studies at Lancaster University, where he chairs the Department of Religious Studies. He studied history at the University of Reading, where he received his B.A. in 1970. His Master's degree in Theology is from the University of Bristol. His doctorate is from the

University of Leeds, with a thesis on contemporary thought in Soto Buddhism. From 1984 to 1991 he lived in Japan and taught at several different universities. He is author or coauthor of six books and coeditor of six others. His recent writings have focused on current Japanese culture, with a special interest in the cult of Aum Shinrikyô.

HUSTON SMITH is Thomas J. Watson Professor of Religion and Distinguished Adjunct Professor of Philosophy Emeritus at Syracuse University. For the past three years he has served as Visiting Professor of Religious Studies at the University of California, Berkeley. His book *The World's Religions* (formerly *The Religions of Man*) has been for thirty years the most widely used textbook for courses in world religions and has sold over 1.5 million copies. He is also the author of such books as *Beyond the Post-Modern Mind; Essays on World Religion; Forgotten Truth;* and (with David Griffin) *Primordial Truth and Postmodern Theology*.

Introduction

ANNA LÄNNSTRÖM

The program brochures for the lecture series on "Promise and Peril: The Paradox of Religion as Resource and Threat" arrived in our office on September 12, 2001. I had thought that the title was clever and current when Lee Rouner conceived it a few months earlier. On September 12, I found it terrifyingly prophetic. The television images of the day before had illustrated the threat of religion so clearly and powerfully that they induced nightmares for months to come, adding to the already familiar fears about other religious conflicts in the world: Catholics and Protestants in Northern Ireland, Jews and Muslims in Israel and Palestine, Hindus and Muslims in India and Pakistan, Buddhists and Hindus in Sri Lanka, and so on. Indeed, the images were so powerful that I found it difficult to remember what the promise of religion was supposed to be.

After witnessing an atrocious act of religious violence, it is tempting to defend religion by denying that the violence was religious, suggesting that those who kill and injure in the name of Islam or Christianity simply have misunderstood their sacred books. We like to believe that true religion is peaceful and compassionate and not aggressive or hurtful. And, indeed, it should be. However, as some of the authors in this volume note, religious practice often fails to live up to our ideals of compassion, and so do our sacred books. The Bible advises us to turn the other cheek but it also advocates taking an eye for an eye, and the Hindu Rig Veda celebrates war. While many religious authorities advocate peace, others regard at least some violence as holy.

The authors in this volume recognize that because religion is ambiguous, it cannot by itself lead people towards compassion and away from violence. Thus, they ask: How do we realize the promise of religion while avoiding the peril of its darker side? How do we prevent fundamentalism from turning violent, and how do we draw upon what is compassionate and good in the religious beliefs on both sides to negotiate a lasting peace in the Middle East, in South Asia, and in Northern Ireland? How do we make sure that religion fosters more Gandhis and Mother Theresas and fewer Mohammed Attas?

The book's first section is entitled Religion and Politics. In "What Is Fundamentalism?" Karen Armstrong argues that in order to make the world safer, we must understand what fundamentalism is and why so many fundamentalists are so angry. *Fundamentalism* has come to refer to groups within various religions that revolt against modern secular society. It develops in reaction to Western-like societies in which politics is separated from religion and where religion seems to be placed on the sidelines. Thus, Armstrong notes, it originates in the belief that modern secular society wants to eliminate religion and that religion therefore must be defended. She points out that this belief has often been confirmed by the actions of secular governments—for example, by Ataturk in Turkey closing the traditional Islamic universities and by the Shahs' soldiers in Iran tearing off women's veils in zealous attempts to discourage non-Western dress.

Armstrong stresses that fundamentalism rarely is violent and that most fundamentalists are not terrorists. However, because fundamentalists often believe that they are fighting for survival, they can turn militant, especially if there already is conflict in the region. And, as Armstrong points out, the more threatened they feel, the more extreme is their reaction likely to be.

So, Armstrong asks, what should we do about fundamentalism? It is not going to disappear. Because it sometimes is dangerous, it cannot be ignored. Violent suppression has not worked and has in fact made fundamentalism more extreme and more dangerous. For example, Armstrong argues, Sayyid Qutb, who later became the mentor of Bin Laden and most other Sunni fundamentalists, was a moderate liberal when Egypt's secular government threw him into prison without trial. His prison experience taught him to see secularism as evil, and he decided that armed struggle is necessary to defend the faith. So how can we prevent fundamentalism from turning violent? Armstrong suggests that the best way to prevent fundamentalist violence is to start by paying attention to the fear and anger that have inspired fundamentalism and by trying to understand what motivates and angers them.

The peril of fundamentalism is clear, but Armstrong reminds us that it also carries some promise. Most importantly, she suggests, fundamentalism can ease the transition to modernity. For example, the Islamic revolution in Iran increased the power of parliament, thus bringing Iran closer to a Western democracy, and it was able to introduce the notion of a strong parliament as an Islamic idea rather than as something Western and alien.

Marc Gopin explores the role of religion in peacemaking in "Jewish-Islamic Negotiations in Israel and Palestine: A Participant Observer's Critical Analysis." He argues that traditional peacemaking focuses solely on rational negotiation and that it ignores the emotional side of human nature. In places of ongoing conflict where deep injuries have occurred, this does not work because people are too angry and hurt to engage in rational negotiations. In addition, the peacemakers often become emotionally engaged themselves and are unable to show what Gopin calls "radical empathy" with both sides. In such situations, Gopin argues, it is necessary to begin by addressing people's anger and pain, and he suggests that religion can play a valuable role here.

Gopin notes that religion often is an element in conflict, and that it has inspired terrible acts of violence. On the other hand, it has also inspired serious and successful peacemaking. How then can we make religion inspire peacemaking rather than war? Gopin stresses that we must start by taking religious myths, metaphors, and rituals seriously, noticing that they have great power. He suggests that we might, for example, arrange joint religious rituals for mourning the dead on both sides or for honoring the religious scriptures of both sides. In Israel, all sides, including the negotiator, must understand what significance the Temple Mount/*harem-al-sherif* has for Jews and for Muslims, why it is so important, and how use and neglect of this symbol and others like it can aid or thwart the peace process. After such beginnings, Gopin suggests, we can embark on a slow process of change and healing through shared rituals, study, and mourning. He stresses that while formal negotiations should accompany this process, they can never replace it.

Gerald James Larson discusses the volatile situation in South Asia in "Nuclearization in the South Asian Region: Interactions between Pakistan and India." He argues that two attitudes about religion compete among Muslims and Hindus in India and Pakistan. The Partition Mindset, named after the 1947 partition of India, resists attempts at dialogue and mutual understanding, refusing to try to harmonize

Muslim and Hindu ideas and instead shutting out the other. In contrast, the Discourse Mindset favors dialogue and synthesis between the two religions and countries. In Larson's view, the most important question in South Asia today is whether or not the Partition Mindset will continue to dominate each of the two religious traditions.

That question grew even more urgent when India and then Pakistan became openly declared nuclear powers in 1998. What was the motivation for nuclearization? Larson suggests that while the reasons are complex, three stand out. Becoming a nuclear power was intended to deter attack from others; to be a source of national pride, drawing attention away from poverty and social deprivation; and to stabilize the political situation in South Asia. Larson notes that these reasons all appear wrongheaded. If anything, nuclearization seems to have encouraged terrorist activity and warfare along the border between the two countries, and the region appears more volatile than ever. And while the nuclear weapons might have distracted people, the fundamental problem of poverty is still very much present.

Larson suggests that the dominant Partition Mindset has prevented self-examination as well as interfaith dialogue, and thus has encouraged nuclearization. However, the solution is not to abandon religion. Rather, Larson argues, Indians and Pakistanis must discuss their respective religious views with each other and begin to understand the other side. That is, the Discourse Mindset must gain ascendance. If this does not happen, if the Partition Mindset remains in power, the consequences can be disastrous.

In "State-Religion Partnership: Boon or Curse?" Bhikhu Parekh argues that the state should provide public funds for religious groups that provide education and other social services, assuming that they meet established criteria and follow applicable government rules. This is so because religious and other volunteer groups have strengths that the state lacks. For example, he points out, they often have a long history of providing charity, and they are good at motivating people and at building close personal relationships with their clients.

So what about religious schools? Should they exist, and should they be publicly funded? Parekh answers that they should be permitted to exist as long as they do not cause public harm, and that they should be publicly funded if they promote public goods. He argues that there are several reasons why religious schools should be funded: First, doing so widens the range of available options, which a liberal society should do. Second, religious schools help foster diversity of ways of thinking and living, and thus make society livelier and richer. Third, competition in education is generally good because it provides data indicating what pedagogies work best. Fourth, permitting religious schools avoids a state monopoly on education. Fifth, education should promote worthwhile social, moral, and spiritual goals. Religious schools sometimes do this better than state schools. Finally, because the state funds other schools, refusing to fund religious schools that offer an equally good education would constitute discrimination.

But don't religious schools promote intolerance and discourage critical thinking? Parekh argues that the state should address this concern by laying a basic curriculum and insisting that all schools must promote important values, such as respect for fellow human beings, equality, and tolerance of differences. If schools are not willing to follow these guidelines, Parekh argues, the state is entitled to withhold funding and sometimes even to close the school.

The second section of the book is called Religion in Itself. In "Awe as Promise and Peril: The Entheogenic Evidence," Huston Smith discusses the use of drugs to occasion religious experiences. He notes that contemporary religions tend to describe encounters with God as involving love and bliss and argues that this is misleading. The encounter with the divine is primarily awe-inspiring; that is, it evokes fascination and fear. The divine both draws us toward it and frightens us away. The God of the Bible loves us, but he is also terrifying.

How then do we discover what awe really is? Smith argues that entheogens (commonly known as psychedelics) can occasion mystical experiences which involve awe, and he supports his claim in part through reference to his own experiences with entheogens. On one hand, the experience is of a world beyond language, one of visions and stillness. On the other hand, it induces fear, a sense of complete isolation in the universe, and a conviction that life is completely meaningless.

Smith notes that drug taking has its perils, including addiction, organic and behavioral toxicity, and psychological and spiritual harm. However, entheogens can also improve our understanding of how God works in the world. Indeed, Smith suggests, many revelations in religious history may have been occasioned by entheogens or by physical exhaustion or hunger. Furthermore, they might help religion regain the importance it ought to have in public life; once people have seen God, they will no longer be tempted to confuse physical reality with reality as a whole.

If we can use drugs or starvation to induce mystical and religious experiences, does that not suggest that such experiences are mere hallucinations? Reductionism says yes; Smith says no. He suggests that even if the drug occasions the experience, there is no reason to assume that it causes it and that the reductionist view relies upon unproven metaphysical assertions about the nature of the mind. Since science has not disproved the possibility of a transcendent reality, Smith concludes, we have no reason to insist that there is none.

In "Killing for Salvation: Aum Shinrikyô and the Perils of Religion," Ian Reader examines Aum Shinrikyô, the cult that was responsible for the Tokyo subway attack in 1995. How, Reader asks, did its originally idealistic members come to believe that they were justified in killing? How did Aum cease being Promise and become Peril? And what role did religion play in this process? In Japan at the time, some argued that because Aum engaged in such horrid acts, it could not be a religion. Reader replies that Aum was both a religion and guilty of mass murder. Indeed, he argues, some of its religious beliefs motivated its actions.

Following Hinduism, the founder of Aum, Asahara, taught that the karma we accumulate through our actions determines our fate after death. He also taught that the world is facing destruction because we have accumulated so much bad karma. He suggested that it could be saved only it were transformed spiritually before the end of the century, if all people were to become members of Aum. However, he became increasingly disillusioned. People did not seem to want to save the world. Instead, Reader shows, Aum faced hostility from parents whose children had joined the movement, from communities in which they wanted to build communes, and from voters who laughed them out of politics. And the end of the century was approaching.

In 1988, Reader notes, Aum came to believe that advanced spiritual beings like the leaders of Aum should save sinners by killing them. This new belief justified Asahara's decision to have a disciple killed, after the disciple threatened to tell the authorities about a death that had occurred during austerities and had been covered up. Asahara argued that the murder allowed the disciple to avoid the bad karma of a betrayal. But, as Reader points out, the new belief was also supported by holy texts, more precisely by Buddhist texts which state that a guru might save a man by killing him before he sins. Over the next few years, Reader shows, Asahara became increasingly convinced that humanity could be saved only by being killed, and Aum finally turned to attempts at mass destruction.

To what extent should we attribute Asahara's development to his religious views? Reader stresses that it was very easy for Asahara to find religious teachings that fitted or reinforced his world views. Perhaps Asahara misused the texts. However, the basic problem and strength of religious traditions and texts is that they admit various very different interpretations. Thus, Reader argues, the study of Aum's descent into violence teaches us that symbolic texts can be interpreted literally and that they then may inspire violence.

In "Moral Paradoxes in Hinduism," Wendy Doniger argues that Hinduism contains a series of moral paradoxes, and she suggests that they all are both dangerous and promising. One of the paradoxes is between monism and pluralism. The Rig Veda allows a number of gods to coexist. The Upanishads, on the other hand, suggest that there ultimately only is one god and, indeed, only one thing. Doniger argues that this paradox is linked to the paradox of whether right belief or right action matters. Monistic thinkers often suggest that while people may act as they like, there is only one right belief. Pluralistic thinkers, in contrast, tend to permit many beliefs and even many religions but believe that rituals and social behavior must be performed in the correct manner. Both views can lead to religious persecution and killings.

Monism and pluralism are also involved in the conflict between renunciation and worldliness. Early Indian tradition suggests that there are three human goals—piety, profit, and pleasure (*dharma, artha,* and *kama*). But around the sixth century B.C.E., a fourth goal, salvation (*moksha*), was added. How then are these goals to be reconciled? Ought one withdraw from the world or engage in it? A pluralistic solution, where the goals are treated as separate but equal, is sometimes suggested. However, Doniger argues, the ultimate Hindu solution to this problem was monistic; escape from the world is the highest goal. And, she argues, this solution is dangerous because it draws attention away from morality and the need for social change. If we withdraw from the world, we do not attempt to improve it.

Doniger notes that the role of morality is also undermined by the paradox of divine sport (*lila*) and ethical action. The Upanishads suggest that the universe is an expression of divine play. What then is the role of ethics? If all is a game, how can ethics matter?

Finally, Hinduism is thought to be nonviolent but, as Doniger notes, India erupts in killing and religious violence again and again. She points out that it is a mistake to assume that Hinduism is nonviolent. It is true that Gandhi stressed nonviolence (*ahimsa*), but the Rig Veda and many other classical Indian texts revere war. Other texts like the Laws of Manu justify certain killings by suggesting that they can be considered nonviolent for ethical purposes. Doniger suggests that the failure of nonviolence in India was in part due to the failure of taking this older tradition into account.

Many of the essays in this volume stress that we fear what is foreign and strange. In areas of conflict, people learn to fear the other side when they are very young. This morning's newspaper reports a study in Northern Ireland in which children as young as three expressed fearful and hateful views about the other side, saying that they were "bad people" and that they "smashed windows."* As Catholics and Protestants are almost entirely segregated in schools in Northern Ireland (only 4 percent are in mixed religion schools, the study reports), such views are likely to be deeply rooted by the time people graduate. And of course, as long as the others seem that dangerous and threatening, we feel justified in protecting ourselves by striking first. Why, after all, should we show compassion to those dangerous bad people who smash our windows? A common and crucial theme of the essays in this book is that we need to fight fear and lack of understanding and instead come to understand the others. Dialogue, openness, and understanding can show us that the people of other religions and other nationalities are not as strange, hateful, and dangerous as we thought. And then, there might be room for religion to fulfill its promise.

---

*Boston Globe, 25 June 2002.

PART I

Religion and Politics

What Is Fundamentalism?

KAREN ARMSTRONG

Since September 11, we have all heard a great deal about the dangers of "fundamentalism," and it now seems more important than ever to gain an accurate knowledge of this religious phenomenon, because it has become an ineradicable part of the modern scene. It is often said that the world changed forever on that terrible day, and there is a sense in which this is undoubtedly true. But it is also the case that nothing much has changed. The destruction of the World Trade Center and the Pentagon may have been the most dramatic and murderous fundamentalist acts to date, but the phenomenon of fundamentalism has been with us for almost a century. The signs of this radical disaffection were plain to see long before September 11, but were not taken seriously enough. If we are to build a safer world, it is crucial that we understand what we are up against and the reasons for this lethal rage.

There is a great deal of misinformation floating about, and we must begin by defining what fundamentalism is *not*. First, it should not be equated with religious conservatism. Billy Graham, for example, is not a fundamentalist; he would neither call himself a fundamentalist nor be claimed by the fundamentalist churches as one of their own. The Saudis are traditionalists, but not fundamentalists. Second, fundamentalism should not automatically be linked with violence. Only a tiny proportion of fundamentalists worldwide take part in acts of terror; the rest are simply struggling to live what they regard as a religious life in a world that seems increasingly inimical to faith. Third, fundamentalism is not an exclusively Islamic phenomenon. During the second half of the twentieth century, this type of religiosity emerged in every single major faith tradition, so that we also have fundamentalist Jews, Christians, Hindus, Buddhists, Sikhs, and even fundamentalist Confucians in China. Indeed, Islam was the last of the three monotheistic religions to develop a fundamentalist strain. Finally, fundamentalism is not monolithic. Each fundamentalist movement has developed spontaneously and independently, and there are often significant differences between them, even within the same faith tradition.

So what is fundamentalism? It must be said at the outset that the term is unsatisfactory. It was coined at the beginning of the twentieth century by American Protestants to describe their reform movement, and people of other traditions resent having this Christian term foisted upon them. Nevertheless, like it or not, the term is now used to refer to those groups which have appeared in religions all over the world and whose militant piety bears a strong family resemblance. Fundamentalism is essentially a revolt against modern secular society. Wherever a Western type of polity which separates religion and politics has been established, a fundamentalist movement has sprung up alongside it in protest. Fundamentalists typically tend to withdraw from mainstream society to create enclaves of pure faith. Typical examples are the Ultra-Orthodox Jewish communities in New York or the Bob Jones University in South Carolina. Here fundamentalists build a counterculture, in conscious defiance of the godless world that surrounds them. From these sacred domains some undertake a counteroffensive designed to drag God or religion back to center stage from the sidelines to which they have been relegated in modern secular culture. This campaign is rarely violent. It usually consists of a propaganda or welfare effort. In the United States, the fundamentalist riposte often attempts to reform school textbooks or to get "Christian" candidates elected to government posts. But if there is already conflict in a region, fundamentalism can get sucked into the political whirlpool and develop more extreme methods. This is what has happened in the Middle East. The Arab-Israeli conflict began on both sides as a secular conflict, but after the Six-Day War of 1967 there was a religious revival on both sides, and a religious form of fundamentalist Zionism and various Islamic movements have added a sacred dimension to the political struggle.

The ubiquity of this fundamentalist revolt shows that there is a widespread disappointment with and alienation from modernity. But what is it about the modern world that has provoked such a strong reaction? During the sixteenth century, the peoples of Europe—and later in the American colonies—began to develop a new type of civilization that was without precedent in world history. Instead of basing their economy on a surplus of agricultural produce, as did all premodern cultures, they relied increasingly upon technology and the constant reinvestment of capital, which freed them from the limitations of agrarian society. This demanded radical change at all levels of society—intellectual, political, social, and religious. A wholly new way of thinking became essential, and new forms of government had to evolve to meet these drastically new conditions. It was found, by trial and error, that the best way of creating a productive society was to separate politics and science from the constraints of a religious establishment and to create a democratic polity, bringing such out-groups as the Jews into mainstream society. It took Europe and America some three hundred years to modernize, and the process was wrenching and traumatic, involving bloody revolutions, reigns of terror, brutal holy wars, dictatorships, cruel exploitation of the workforce, despoliation of the countryside, and widespread alienation and anomie. Nevertheless, by the nineteenth century the process was complete and the West had become invincible. We are now witnessing the same kind of upheaval in the developing countries, which are presently undergoing modernization. They also have to face difficulties the West escaped, namely, having to complete the process far too rapidly and having to follow a Western program rather than their own natural dynamic. In addition, as modernization progresses, people find that they cannot be religious in the old way, and they try to find new means of expressing their piety. Fundamentalism is just one of these attempts, and it therefore develops only after a degree of modernization has been achieved. Thus the very first fundamentalist movement emerged in the United States, the showcase of modernity, during the First World War. Fundamentalism in the Islamic world, on the other hand, did not develop until the late 1960s, when some Muslims felt that secular, foreign ideologies like nationalism or socialism had failed them.

Because fundamentalists are primarily concerned with saving their own society, they are not, initially, interested in attacking a foreign foe. Rather, they begin with a critique of their own coreligionists and compatriots. Thus fundamentalism does not represent a clash *between* civilizations, but a clash *within* civilizations and an intrareligious struggle. In the United States, for example, Protestant fundamentalists at first fought the more liberal Christians, who had come to terms with modern conditions, for control of the various denominations. More recently, Hamas militants began by attacking Yasser Arafat and the Palestine Liberation Organization; they wanted the Palestinian movement to be inspired by religion rather than by secular politics. It was only during the first *intifadah* of 1987 that Hamas began to attack Israelis. Similarly Bin Laden began by targeting the Saudi royal family and the secularist governments of such countries as Egypt and Jordan. It was only in 1998 that he turned his attention to the United States, which was supporting rulers whom he regarded as apostates and as traitors to Islam.

Perhaps the most important factor to understand about this widespread religious militancy is that it is rooted in a deep fear of annihilation. Every single fundamentalist movement that I have studied in Judaism, Christianity, and Islam is convinced that modern secular society wants to wipe out religion—even in the United States. Fundamentalists, therefore, believe that they are fighting for survival, and when people feel that their backs are to the wall, some can strike out violently, like a wounded animal. This profound terror of annihilation is not as paranoid as it may at first appear. Jewish fundamentalism gained fresh momentum after the Holocaust. In the Muslim countries, modernization has usually been so accelerated that secularization, the desacralization of politics, has been experienced as an assault. When Mustafa Kemal Ataturk created modern secular Turkey, he closed down all the *madrasahs*, the traditional Islamic universities, and abolished all the Sufi orders, forcing the Sufis underground. He also forced all men and women to wear Western dress. Reformers such as Ataturk wanted their countries to look modern, even though the vast majority of the population had not had a Western education and simply could not understand the new secular institutions and ideologies.

In Iran, the shahs used to make their soldiers walk through the streets with their bayonets out, tearing off women's veils and ripping them to pieces in front of them. In 1935, in Mashad, one of the holiest shrines in Iran, Shah Reza Pahlavi gave his soldiers orders to shoot at unarmed demonstrators who were peacefully protesting against obligatory Western dress. Hundreds of Iranians died that day. In such circumstances, of course, secularization does not seem to liberate religion, as it did in the United States, but rather seems dangerous and wicked. In the days before the Islamic revolution of 1978–79, Shah Muhammad Reza Pahlavi rounded up hundreds of Iranian demonstrators and theology students, exiled some mullahs and tortured others to death, and imprisoned thousands of civilians without trial. Similarly, the main fundamentalist ideology of Sunni Islam, the form of the faith practiced by the majority of Muslims, developed in the concentration camps in Egypt. President Gamal Abdel-Nasser had incarcerated thousands of members of the Muslim Brotherhood in the late 1950s, without trial and often for doing nothing more incriminating than attending a meeting or handing out leaflets. One of these prisoners was Sayyid Qutb, who was executed by Nasser in 1966 and who is the mentor of most Sunni fundamentalists, including Bin Laden. Qutb went into the camp as a moderate and a liberal; he had once been enamored of Western culture and favored secularism. But in these vile prisons, watching the Brothers being executed and subjected to mental and physical torture, and hearing Nasser vowing to relegate Islam to a marginal role in Egypt, he came to regard secularism as a great evil, and developed an ideology of committed armed struggle against this threat to the faith.

Thus fundamentalism usually develops in a symbiotic relationship with a secularism that is experienced as hostile and invasive. Every single fundamentalist movement that I have studied in each of the three monotheistic traditions has developed in response to this type of secularist attack. The more vicious the assault, the more extreme the fundamentalist riposte is likely to be. That is one of the reasons why fundamentalism has been less violent in the United States, where the federal government has not resorted to draconian methods to promote its secularist program. The chief weapon has not been torture but ridicule. When the fundamentalists tried to ban the teaching of evolution in the public schools during the 1925 Scopes Trial, the secular press poured scorn on the fundamentalists, implying that they were irredeemably primitive and could play no useful role in modern America. The journalists ignored the profound fear that lay at the heart of the fundamentalists' mistaken opposition to Darwinism, which had become for them a symbol of the most lethal and immoral aspects of modernity. The result was most unfortunate. Before the Scopes Trial, fundamentalists had tended to be literal in their interpretation of scripture, and what is now known as Creation Science was the pursuit of an eccentric minority. After the Scopes Trial, they became more militantly literal and Creation Science became one of the hallmarks of true faith. Before the Scopes Trial, fundamentalists had often been at the left of the political spectrum and had been willing to work alongside liberal Christians and socialists in the slums of the newly industrialized cities. After the Scopes Trial, fundamentalists swung to the far right, where they have remained. When liberals deplore the development and persistence of fundamentalism both in their own societies and worldwide, they should be aware that the excesses of secularists all too often have been responsible for this radical alienation.

Fundamentalism seems outrageous because it appears to be a deliberate attempt to deny progress and to turn the clock back. The media often depict fundamentalists as atavistically wedded to the past, but this is a grave mistake. Fundamentalisms are essentially modern ideologies, which could have taken root in no time other than our own. Protestant fundamentalists, for example, claim to be returning to the original meaning of scripture, but in fact they are reading the Bible in a wholly modern way. When they quote scripture in great detail, citing chapter and verse, they show an intimate knowledge of the Bible that would have been impossible before the modern development of printing made it possible for every Christian to own his or her own Bible and before the modern phenomenon of near universal literacy enabled them to read it. Before the modern period, most people listened to scripture read aloud, usually in a foreign language and in a liturgical setting. As a valuable piece of sacred equipment, the Bible was usually chained up in the churches, and the laity had a very different relationship with their sacred texts. In the premodern period, people in all the major faiths relished highly allegorical and symbolical interpretations of scripture. Jews, Christians, and Muslims all regarded their scriptural texts as the Word of God and, therefore, infinite. It was impossible for a passage to be tied down to a single interpretation. But today many read the Bible or the Qur'an for information, treating them as secular texts or holy encyclopedias containing facts about God. This literal approach to scripture is wholly new and it is a product of our modern society. It would have been very surprising to such luminaries as Thomas Aquinas, Martin Luther, and John Calvin.

In the same way, Sayyid Qutb was essentially a man of the 1960s. He preached an Islamic liberation theology: because God alone is sovereign, Muslims need obey no human authority whatsoever. Similarly, Ayatollah Khomeini was a typical Third World politician, concerned for the poor and for justice, and determined to throw off the shackles of Western imperialism. Where the other ayatollahs usually spoke in a pedantic, remote style, Khomeini—like any modern politician—was a populist who spoke directly to the people in terms that they could understand. The media were completely mistaken in presenting him as a throwback to the Middle Ages. What he did with Shi'ite Islam was as revolutionary as it would be for the pope to abolish the Mass. It is true that fundamentalists often look back to a Golden Age, when they believe that people were true to the faith, but their policies and ideals are essentially those of the modern world. As such, fundamentalism is not an atavistic return to the past, but part of the modern scene and here to stay. A refusal to recognize this fact is a failure to take fundamentalism seriously, and, after September 11, we can no longer afford such attitudes of patrician superiority.

Because fundamentalisms are essentially modern movements, they can also be modernizing. History shows that religion has often enabled people to make an easier transition out of what could have been a painful rite of passage to modernity. At the time of the American War of Independence against Britain, a modernizing conflict, very few of the colonists could identify with the Enlightenment philosophy of the Founding Fathers. On the contrary, most were Calvinists and regarded the deism and secularism of such leaders as Thomas Jefferson as satanic. Very few were capable of reading the British philosopher John Locke, whose ideas helped to inspire the Declaration of Independence. But they were able to evolve their own Calvinist revolutionary ideology. This ideology enabled them to fight alongside the secularists for their liberty, a word that had become saturated with religious meaning in America ever since the First Great Awakening (1734–40). Similarly, after the War of Independence, the prophets of the Second Great Awakening on the frontiers used the Gospels to demand far greater liberty and a greater share in the democratic process than such presidents as John Adams had envisaged. Preachers such as Lorenzo Dow, Elias Smith, and James O'Kelly may have looked like Old Testament prophets, with their flowing hair and wild gestures. But they quoted Thomas Jefferson or Tom Paine alongside the New Testament, had been radicalized by the War of Independence, and, like the fundamentalist leaders, were men of their time. They enabled their followers to appropriate modern ideals in a package that made far more sense to them than the philosophy of the Enlightenment.

We can see a similar process in some contemporary fundamentalist movements. Not all are modernizing, of course. The Taliban, for example, scarcely merit the name *fundamentalist*. They are in large part a product of the Cold War in Afghanistan and the chaos that followed the Soviet invasion of Afghanistan. They have no seriously Islamic ideology that could compare with that of a Khomeini, and are not progressive. But the case of Iran is striking. Before the Islamic Revolution, Iranians had never had representational government. A Constitutional Revolution in 1906 had forced the shahs to establish a Majlis (a parliament) but it was never permitted to function freely, either under the British or under the Pahlavi shahs. After the Islamic Revolution, the Majlis has become a regular part of Iranian political life. It is far from perfect, of course, but it took Western countries many years to develop true democracy and total enfranchisement. At the end of his life, Khomeini was trying to curb the influence of the conservative clerics on the Council of Guardians, and give more power to the Majlis. He also urged the Guardians not to meddle with the economy or other matters about which they were ignorant: government had to be free to function without these religious constraints.[1] He had realized that the only way to run a modern state was to democratize and to achieve a certain separation of religion and state. With his permission, the Speaker of the Majlis, Hashemi Rafsanjani, called for a Shi'ite democracy, which would be present in Iran "in a form better than the West," because it was rooted in God.[2] As in the West, the needs of the modern state had propelled Iran toward a democratic polity. Democracy, however, did not come as a foreign, alien import, but in an Islamic package, to which the people could relate and link with their own Shi'i traditions. The democratizing process continues under President Khatemi.

One can say the same about the voluntary adoption of Islamic dress by some women in such countries as Egypt. A survey conducted in Egypt in 1982 showed that a remarkably high proportion of veiled women held progressive views on gender issues.[3] Further, the clothing worn by these women is not the garb worn by their grandmothers. Rather, it is a new fashion, which resembles Western styles (apart from the long sleeves and skirts). It could be seen as a "halfway house" and as the uniform of transition to modern society. A large number of the women who opt for Islamic dress are the first members of their families to have advanced beyond basic literacy and to attend a university. They often come from the rural areas of Egypt, which are deeply traditional and very different from modern cities like Cairo. The familiar dress, and the Islamic lifestyle that goes with it, proclaims their upward mobility, but it also provides some continuity with what they had worn before. It enables them to make what could have been a traumatic rite of passage more easily and peacefully. Yet again, perhaps, religion is helping people to cross over from a conventional to a more modern lifestyle and ideology, providing another modernizing stratagem.[4]

The fundamentalists have had some success in restoring religion to the center of public life. In the middle of the twentieth century, it was generally assumed that secularism was irresistible and that religion would never again play a major role in public life. But the fundamentalist riposte has reversed this process. Zionism began as a defiantly secularist ideology; it was a revolt against religious Judaism. But today no Israeli politician can form a government unless he goes cap in hand to the Orthodox religious parties. Religion has become central to Israeli polity in a way that would have astonished the first Israeli Prime Minister, Ben Gurion. In the United States, the first secular republic in the modern world, presidential candidates must now flaunt their born-again credentials. At the height of the Monica Lewinsky scandal, President Clinton found it necessary to appear on television at a prayer breakfast for the religious leaders of America, weeping and confessing that he had sinned. This event astonished Europeans, who have resisted the religious revival and are still deeply wedded to secularism. In Egypt, Islam is now as popular among the people as Nasserism was during the 1950s and 1960s. After September 11, it is clear that we must recognize that religion is still a force to be reckoned with.

But September 11 shows the hideous dangers of fundamentalist piety. Without exception, all the world faiths teach that the one single test of any religious experience or ideology is whether or not it issues in practical compassion. The prophets of Israel, the New Testament, and the Qur'an all insist that any faith that neglects the demands of social justice, refuses to recognize the inviolable rights of others, and does not honor the sanctity of human life is a travesty. You can have faith that moves mountains, but if you lack charity it is worth nothing. But fundamentalists have usually ignored this crucial insight. Because they feel so threatened by the secular ideal and polity that is dominant in their society, and which has often been experienced as a lethal assault on faith, they neglect the exhortations to compassion and emphasize the more intransigent elements that also exist in all our traditions. This is a crisis, and thus, they believe, a more hard-line approach is essential. Thus fundamentalists distort the very religion they are trying to defend and protect by taking hostages, destroying other people's homes or shrines, gunning down their presidents, shooting doctors and nurses who work in abortion clinics, initiating suicide attacks, or simply berating and deriding the position and desires of others. Fundamentalism, therefore, may have achieved some success; however, it represents a major defeat for religion.

But what is the way forward? Secularists once imagined that religion would modestly retreat to the sidelines and confine itself to private life, but fundamentalism is not going to disappear. September 11 has shown the truly lethal potential of this type of faith, which uses such concepts as *God* to give a seal of absolute, sacred approval to our worst prejudice and hatred. History shows that it is no use ignoring fundamentalism; it is here to stay. And in Judaism, Christianity, and Islam, at least, it is becoming more extreme. Even in the United States, Protestant militants have gone far beyond Jerry Falwell and his Moral Majority. The Reconstructionist Movement, headed by Gary North and Rousas John Rushdoony, expects the imminent destruction of the federal democratic government of the United States by God, and its adherents are training themselves to take over when this secular humanist state is destroyed.[5] The blazing towers of the World Trade Center would not be alien to their vision. Christian Identity, a fascist group, has rejected traditional fundamentalism altogether in a far more extreme vision: they predict a new holocaust in which the white race and the United States will be annihilated.[6]

Theologies of hatred and extremism are not confined to the Islamic world, and we can no longer ignore the disaffection and fear that have inspired these fearful apocalyptic fantasies. History shows that violent suppression of fundamentalist movements only makes them more extreme. Because fundamentalists fear that secularists want to destroy them, aggressive and military action will only serve to exacerbate this fear, and may cause it to spill over into ungovernable rage. It is also dangerous to adopt short-sighted policies that seek to exploit fundamentalist movements to serve our own interests. Thus President Anwar al-Sadat initially courted the Islamist groups that were developing in the universities of Egypt during the 1970s, in order to build a power base against those who remained loyal to Nasserism. They proved to be a Frankensteinian monster that killed him. Israel originally supported and funded Hamas in order to undermine Arafat and the Palestine Liberation Organization, and the United States encouraged and supported Bin Laden and his like to fight their Cold War battles in Afghanistan.

Policies of suppression and exploitation fail because they do not show the compassion and respect that are the ideals of our modern secular society. They do not recognize the pain and fear that, if ignored and allowed to fester, can occasionally result in the kind of atrocity that we saw on September 11. Fundamentalism is not confined to the "other" civilizations; a dangerous gulf has appeared dividing each society against itself. Even in Europe, where religion is not a major force in politics, right-wing movements which espouse a fascist ideology have sprouted up and soccer hooliganism has erupted in the United Kingdom. These trends show exactly the same blend of emotions that fuels many of the fundamentalist movements: a pent-up rage and helplessness, a hatred and a pernicious view of the "other," a desire to belong to a clearly defined group, and a profound feeling of inferiority and alienation from mainstream secular humanism. The first step must be to look beneath the bizarre and often repulsive ideology of these movements in order to discern the disquiet and anger that lie at their roots. We must no longer deride these theologies as the fantasies of a lunatic fringe, but rather learn to decode their ideas. Only then can we deal creatively with these fears and anxieties that, as we have seen, no society can safely dismiss.

NOTES

1. Foreign Broadcasting and Information Service [FBIS], 24 December 1987 and 7 January 1988.

2. FBIS, 19 January 1988.

3. Leila Ahmed, *Women and Gender in Islam: Historical Roots of a Modern Debate* (New Haven, Conn.: Yale University Press, 1992), pp. 226–28.

4. Ibid., pp. 220–25.

5. Nancy T. Ammerman, "North American Protestant Fundamentalism," in *Fundamentalisms Observed,* ed. Martin Marty and R. Scott Appleby (Chicago: University of Chicago Press, 1991), pp. 49–53; Michael Lienesch, *Redeeming America: Piety and Politics in the New Christian Right* (Chapel Hill: University of North Carolina Press, 1993), p. 226.

6. Michael Barkun, *Religion and the Racist Right: The Origins of the Christian Identity Movement* (Chapel Hill: University of North Carolina Press, 1994).

Jewish-Islamic Negotiations in Israel and Palestine: A Participant Observer's Critical Analysis

MARC GOPIN

I began my journey as a scholar and practitioner of peacemaking by studying religious ethics. As I became a practitioner, I found that the abstract study of the subject did not easily translate into practice because the hardest details of conflict scenarios defy the categories of traditional ethical choices. The field of culture and conflict resolution explores contradictory human traits: our propensities for peace and violence, pro-social and anti-social values, compassion and demonic barbarism. How is it possible for us to have these paradoxical capacities at the same time? This question is basic to many branches of social and psychological inquiry and to anthropological studies of societies around the world.

Conflict analysis and conflict resolution draw from anthropology, social psychology, and sociology. At its early inception—only about ten years ago—anthropologists were the troublemakers, raising basic doubts about the arrogance of Western models of analysis and intervention. In addition, anthropologists and political scientists like Marc Ross and Kevin Avruch noted that conflict analysis and resolution, as well as diplomacy and negotiation, were inadequately addressing the "nonrational" or emotional side of human experience.[1] This "nonrational" side was only considered as a problem to be solved, something to be suppressed or removed so that one could get on with the real business of negotiation. Such evasion of the nonrational factors still dominates the style, character, and substance of thousands of negotiations around the world, especially those involving treaties and basic state-to-state relations, but also the attempts to solve these intractable conflicts—conflicts that go on for generations.

In intractable conflicts, methods focused on rational negotiation help partially. However, at other times these same methods have failed miserably. As I studied the research and compared it to the empirical reality of human experience in deadly conflict, I discovered some extraordinary discrepancies. I saw that my students who came from cultural conflicts around the world often disliked these rationally focused methods. My own experiences with family conflict and lifelong exposure to the Israeli-Arab or Jewish-Arab conflict showed that these methods were never applicable to anyone but highly educated negotiators, and certainly not to those members of my extended family and community who were heavily invested in the Middle East conflict. Not only were these methods failing, they were actually causing many problems because they raised false hopes of settlement.[2]

It started to become clear that the first and second parties in conflict do what they are supposed to be doing. In other words, they engage in preestablished patterns, including cycles of violence such as escalation, demonization, or slow and steady mimesis where both parties end up resembling each other. The third parties and the bystanders have the greatest potential to act creatively. But in the literature they are mostly treated as if they are disembodied observers. In fact, their unawareness of their own biases and emotional reactions to the conflicts at hand makes them singularly unprepared to help the first and second parties achieve the greater level of self-awareness that is presupposed by any rational negotiation.

It was not until Vamik Volkan and others began studying the deeper aspects of psychology that we started to see that in places of deep injury, the resulting strong emotions undermined ordinary negotiations.[3] In such situations, it is necessary to start by working with the emotional side of the human experience in a way that allows people eventually to wake up from these unconscious, primal processes. Only after the emotional side has been addressed would the parties be able to get to more interest-based negotiations and reach rational compromises. We had to find a way to help large populations work through their emotions, with the help of good enough leadership. This was especially crucial if that leadership wanted political maneuvering room to make difficult compromises called for by rational investigation.

Of course, if civility, covenants, and social contracts are already firmly in place, it is unnecessary to revisit life histories or ancestral traumas before negotiating a treaty over, say, rights to various fisheries.

However, when human relations break down to such a severe degree that no rational negotiations are working, the emotional side must be addressed first.

In this context I realized that religion was a dark abyss in academic research on conflict, partly because it has been compartmentalized within the study of human phenomena and within the university. Therefore, it is not easily subject to cross-disciplinary investigations. There are a number of reasons for this—including the very understandable human biases of social science and social scientists. The realm of religion is a realm of trouble for people who have escaped from repressive religious structures. This dark fear of religion has absurd results. For example, before it became obvious that religion played a major role in the Middle Eastern suicide bombings it was dismissed as irrelevant to the power politics or the material interests of all parties. Even after the best hope for peace to come along in a generation, Anwar Sadat, was assassinated, religion was still dismissed. Then Yitshak Rabin, the next great hope, was assassinated. Still religion had to be irrelevant. Then wave after wave of religiously inspired suicide bombs rocked Jerusalem and brought about Netanyahu's election and his stalling of the peace process. Still nothing. On September 11, 2001, all this changed. If one spoke about religion as a pathology or a problem, vast audiences would listen. On the other hand, if religion was presented as a solution, many perceived it as a dangerous threat to public order.

Religion also seems to be what is at stake in the contemporary global struggle for public space between many fundamentalisms around the world and the realms of secular culture. While millions of religious people are perfectly comfortable with the public space being shared or being exclusively secular, millions of others are determined to take back that space by manipulation, by elections, or by violence, in the name of religion.

Arriving at a constructive relationship between religion, diplomacy, and third-party intervention has not been easy. In fact, the religious element, as one element among many in its relation to conflict analysis and diplomatic efforts, has constantly been challenged. Scott Appleby and I have explored some of these challenges.[4] We have identified and established what Appleby has called "the ambivalence of the sacred." On one hand, in the hands of people like Gandhi, Martin Luther King, and the Dalai Lama, religion has inspired the most aggressive and successful forms of peacemaking that the world has seen. Their vision has prevented the suffering and death of millions of people. On the other hand, millions of people have died because of religiously inspired violence.

The ambivalence of the sacred can also be found in the texts. Peaceful laws, such as the prohibition against killing and the duty to help one's enemy, can be found in the Books of Exodus and Deuteronomy, for example.[5] Nevertheless, the same texts refer to the duty of killing every man, woman, and child who belongs to the Canaanite nations.[6] Likewise, some of the most beautiful poems of medieval saints, such as Bernard of Clairvaux, also report on glorious visions of the bloody streets of Jerusalem during the Crusades.[7]

Today, one can refer to letters like the one written by Mohammed Atta, one of the September 11 hijackers.[8] His last testament does not allude to revenge or anger but to the purity and preparations needed just before the encounter with God. It is important because Atta is referring to the preparation of a number of individuals who will arrive at the heavenly encounter only after murdering thousands of civilians. These examples help us understand that the ambivalence of the sacred refers to the primal forces of the human being. These primal forces include both an incredible capacity for barbarity and a passionate capacity for altruism, surrender, care, empathy, and self-sacrifice. Throughout history, all of these forces have flowed within religious experience. Sometimes they actually flow together, as, for example, when one who advocates or practices mass murder prepares himself for the ultimate act of altruism, giving his life for the greater glory of God and the sanctification of God's name.

We need to examine these texts and moments in history carefully, asking whether this ambivalence can be shaped and moved in the direction of pro-social values and behavior, or whether secular repression of religious enthusiasm is the only way to safeguard innocent victims of war. Furthermore, can the already formulated pro-social values of many religious systems merge creatively with the widespread commitments to freedom, democracy, civil rights, and universal human rights as the basis of civil societies of the future? Such commitments form part of an evolving "secular religion of the human community," which has been gradually accepted by many. These universal principles have emerged in the same powerful and widespread way as the countervailing religious extremist trends that move in the opposite direction.

Political scientists, anthropologists, and psychologists have explored how the two countervailing trends can coexist. For example, Marc Ross offers interesting insights about Northern Ireland.[9] He has focused on the symbolic aspects of the Protestant marches. There are a number of reasons that lead authors to explore the intricacies and secrets of these symbols. Myths, symbols, metaphors, and rituals are the way in which people often arrive at a violent hell of their own making. Consequently, I argue that they will provide the ways in which to help people emerge from that violent hell. Because they ignore the emotional power of myth and symbol, the elite rational negotiations that take place in faraway castles or in London cannot really affect the Irish marches. We can develop better approaches by using the same symbols and alluding to the same myths. For example, some have tried creating alternative marches. Many alternative efforts have been experimented with in Ireland, and they tend to focus on work that addresses the deeper injuries of the conflict and the cultural roots of both conflict and peacemaking. These practices have shaped individuals at the negotiation tables who have now become familiar with the importance of the symbolic processes of change.

These religious and symbolic frameworks are a useful introduction to the question of Israel and Palestine. The Temple Mount/*haram-al-sherif* is a powerful symbol capable of destroying many of the processes that took place at Camp David. The one square mile of the Temple Mount, home to the vestiges of both ancient Jewish Temples, the holiest site in the world for Judaism, is the third holiest site of Islam with the magnificent Al Aqsa mosque, and also the Temple site through which Jesus walked and made his pronouncements. This area is at the core of the imaginative and symbolic conflict of Palestinians and Israelis. It is their umbilical cord to legitimate claim upon the land itself. It is their treasure and their comfort in the face of massive historical losses. This one symbolic space is also intimately connected to billions of people around the world who are rooted in the monotheistic cultures of the Abrahamic faiths.

This conflict is so intractable because there are no third parties who stand outside it. There are, of course, third parties—such as Americans, Protestants, Catholics, or secular people—who *think* that they are not part of this conflict. Nevertheless, all of these groups come from monotheistic cultures that are deeply related to this ancient spot in Jerusalem. It is a primal place of birth, of loss, and of longing—as all birthplaces are. The fights over legitimacy on the Temple Mount and the denial of Jewish historical connection to this spot have roused intense anger among ordinary people as well as inside the failed negotiations of Camp David in 2000.

So far very few people in this conflict, both unofficial and official, have demonstrated the capacity to listen to the depths of this story, the mythic/cultural/religious significance of story per se, and the pathologies of all sides of this conflict embedded in their particular memory. Even worse, they assume that the lack of conversation about these older strata of consciousness suggests that they are not important.

I know a prominent Palestinian liberal intellectual in Eastern Jerusalem who engaged in many discussions between Muslims and Jews during the Oslo years. It was not until recently that this scholar realized that the Temple Mount was truly important to most Jews. There might be many reasons for his misunderstanding. A simple one could be that his interlocutors did not realize the importance until the issue was brought to the table. In other words, no one had previously understood the importance of Old Jerusalem. His claim is that in numerous conversations even religious Jews downplayed its importance to him, and so he claims that the Palestinian side did not realize that denying Jewish sovereignty on or rights to this spot would destroy so much at Camp David. But the Jews, and even the Americans, would argue that the outrageous denial of Jewish presence on that ancient site was evidence of a larger unwillingness to truly recognize Israel's right to existence. Why were these things not discussed deeply for thirteen years of Oslo? Why were the surprises saved for the last minute?

After thirteen years of Oslo, billions of dollars of projects that went down the drain in corruption, twelve police forces ending up in the West Bank, absolutely no serious trust has been built. There has not been a single truly honest conversation on the most primal space of longing, mourning, rage, and aspirations that are embodied in that one square kilometer. There were endless plans for that one spot, and for the Old City, and for Jerusalem as such. Many clever plans were introduced by very smart people, some officials and some academics. But I could not believe my ears when I realized that those conversations were never cross-cultural. They never touched the bi-communal depths of memory and longing, past, present and future, never probed the linkage of existence, meaning, and survival and the symbol of this one place. And so they were unprepared for the moment of truth, the moment in which civilizations choose between war and peace, death and life. This exemplifies how all parties—including the Americans and the Europeans—unconsciously conspired so as not think about these primal spaces, because they did not have a way to deal with it.

My Arab and Jewish religious friends in Israel, who are for the most part ignored politically but who do have personal linkages to Israeli and Palestinian officials, sit every Friday morning overlooking the Temple Mount. They are Jews, Muslims, Sufis, and Christians who sit there for an hour while chanting *shalom* and *salaam,* and sharing hopes and prayers. People come and visit them, and they keep chanting. Do they have an impact on the leadership? No. On the other hand, one would be surprised about how much is and was going on beneath the surface between *this* kind of actors and officials at the highest level. Was it enough to stop the violence? No, not yet. But, at the same time, considering how little financial support and protection there has been for these courageous people, it is remarkable how much impact they have had. Finding and supporting such unusual religious actors, especially those with good political sensibilities, is one of the key tasks of religious peacebuilding.

I travel to Israel often to do something called "active compassionate listening." I have gone with a group called Initiatives of Change, a group that is not perfect, but whose intuitive peacemaking methods are brilliant in creating relationships. And relationship building is the gateway to cultural and religious conflict resolution. For many practitioners of conflict resolution—particularly those who devote attention to conflict transformation and to John Paul Lederach's literature on the Mennonite Model—relationship building is central.[10] These relationships do not mean "dialogue." Instead, they involve gestures, symbols, and deeds. The group I traveled with decided to try this approach in Israel and Palestine, especially because they knew that "dialogue" had previously failed. It had failed because they themselves had difficulty expressing empathy simultaneously with both Arabs and Jews, instead demonizing one side and ignoring the flaws of the other.

Such one-sided approaches to the conflict in Israel are common in the Western world. Some demonize the Jews and deny the dangers inherent in the current expression of the Palestinian Authority, Palestine Liberation Organization, and Islamic terrorism. On the other hand, others demonize the Muslims; they claim that there is nothing wrong with the behavior of the Israel Defense Forces and deny that Israel has contributed to the misery of the Palestinian people. The conflict is exacerbated because external forces strengthen both sides. This represents the dangers of pretending to be a peacemaker. If the peacemakers do not have the discipline of "radical empathy" simultaneously with all sides, they will become part of the problem.

During the visit to Israel we decided to speak to everybody across the spectrum of ethnicity, religion, and education. We engaged in classic "second track diplomacy" involving Haredi and Hasidic rabbis, Sephardi cultural leaders, members of the Israeli Parliament, people in the Israeli Foreign Ministry, Palestinian officials, Palestinian intellectuals, Palestinian activists, Palestinian professors, and even simple Palestinian newlyweds. In the process, I became involved in what we now call "track one and a half diplomacy." This means that we were moving in between these actors on the ground—mostly of a religious nature—and the official elites, such as the Office of the Israeli Prime Minister and the President of the Palestinian Authority.

Another feature of our program is called elicitive peacemaking. Its bottom line is humility and paying careful attention to what people "on the ground" claim is essential for stopping the violence or moving peacemaking forward. I sometimes still disagree with or distance myself from local methods of peacemaking where the evidence seems clear that they are actually doing more harm than good.[11] On the other hand, if I am uncertain about which path to follow I listen very carefully to the advice of local actors.

Some local actors encouraged me to engage in a new peace track which was meant as a parallel peace process—a religious one. These efforts yielded some results. Nevertheless, these results have been completely overshadowed by recent levels of violence and barbarity.

Years were spent working on a "religious peace treaty." A meeting in the winter of 2002 in Alexandria, Egypt, is one of the most recent attempts to revive previous efforts in this regard. Among the signers of this meeting's documents are the Sephardic Chief Rabbi of Israel; the Deputy Foreign Minister of the Israeli government; a Minister of the Palestinian Authority, Talal Seder; the Chief Sheikh of Alazar University, Tantawi; the second in command to the Mufti of Jerusalem; and a number of Christian clerics who are heads of the churches in Israel. Rabbi Menahem Frohman, one of the central proponents of religious peacemaking, also signed the document.

This represents the flowering of much that has been done in the past. Nevertheless, it fell far short of the kind of symbolic and ethical gestures that Rabbi Frohman and I have been advocating. This action focused on a document, and was not nearly strong enough to change people's deeper emotions. However, statements are also important. For all of these leaders to come to the conclusion that the Holy Land is holy to all three faiths, that all must respect the purposes of the Creator, that nobody should shed innocent blood, is a significant achievement. They framed their ideas under the "name of the God who is all mighty, merciful, and compassionate," a line that symbolizes the fusion of Jewish and Islamic prolegomena. It was a remarkable document that unfortunately delivered far too little and arrived far too late to stem the harm done by months and months of barbaric violence.

This kind of interreligious statement is of course not enough to stop the violence. Rather, people of different faiths need to be taught how to stop demonizing the other. This process takes a long time. However, it eventually causes enough shock to the system by involving enough people. Once this shift occurs, there are enough people in the middle to isolate radicals on both sides.

As a follow-up to Alexandria, I have proposed gestures such as joint religious rituals for mourning the dead and expressing sorrow over the loss of sacred life, especially of the innocent children. Consciousness of death infects most conflicts and the rational methods of negotiation do not even begin to address its destructive power within the peacemaking process. These approaches do not acknowledge that people kill and die for generations because of their need to honor the dead, to ensure that they did not die for nothing. Therefore, there is a need for religious and political leaders to mourn and acknowledge— by word and deed—both peoples' losses.

I have also proposed various ways of honoring the Torah and the Qur'an in a very physical and immediate way. This would provide demonstrable evidence symbolizing a "new era" and would seriously affect the perceptions and behavior of religious people on both sides, thereby making it harder for them to drift toward extremist groups and extremist behavior. Mourning the dead and honoring cultural symbols of a group affect a far broader group of people than the devout. The key is to provoke enough change in the middle of both cultures to create a majority for peace and justice.

This process of entering into what I sometimes call "mythic peacemaking" is, indeed, very strange. In 2000, the West Bank rabbi, the Sufi sheikh, some of my other colleagues, and I finally made it into Arafat's office, after experiencing some perilous impediments. I visited Arafat with great misgivings. I know his history. I know how he plays both sides constantly. I also questioned, however, whether he was in full control of his emotions. I still do. I suspect that standard forms of diplomacy and enemy negotiations have not accessed a place in his mind and heart, so that he veers constantly between war and peace. I was moved by local colleagues who felt that it was worth trying where rational methods of negotiations had failed.

Arafat sat with us for hours. We spoke for a long time about a religious and mythic universe that rabbis, sheikhs, and ministers would understand, but which would drive average diplomats crazy. We spoke and dreamed about a Holy Land where there were no states, a kind of nonviolent version of messianic Jewish dreams and Islamic dreams of the Caliphate. In Arafat's mind the real vision was to become the liberator of this Holy Land, a guardian of all three Abrahamic faiths. And I considered it our job to help him find ways politically to be a Salaadin to his people, a liberator and caretaker of the holy places of all three religions—but without violence.

Arafat liked the role that we were offering him—the protector of holy spaces. While we were there, he put us on Palestinian television three times. Now this is the same man that permitted the continuation of Hamas, Al Aqsa brigades, Tanzim, and suicide bombing activity against civilians, including children. He is a man of complete contradiction. Those of us who were there felt that it would not be the first time in history in which unstable leaders need to be moved and cajoled in one direction. We also felt that the rationalist methods had failed completely and would in the future.

As a follow-up to this visit local activists envisioned a group comprised of religious practitioners working together. They wanted this group to help the political leaders move to a different cultural and psychological space. The objective would be to change their attitude with regard to the "enemy."

If we had had a third party such as the United States that really understood the power of cultural gestures and the motivating power of

Western Wall with the old Jewish men. They would say their prayers and I would say mine." In that instant he was letting me know that he did not buy all that nonsense he had spouted at Camp David about Jews having no historical relationship to the Temple Mount. I think that he was offering me something, a religious gesture of acknowledgement and honor, just as I had honored him by mourning his dead and acknowledging the importance of justice in this conflict.

The next day Arafat announced, for the first time after six months of the Intifada, that there should be no killing of civilians. This gesture was eventually rolled over and buried by violent action, counteraction, revenge, retaliation, and punishment. The moment we had created interreligiously, interculturally was gone, dead and buried. But we had proved that such moments are possible, and that they can be multiplied many times. Moments like these represent one step of a whole intercultural process that should slowly allow for a new vision to take place *if* there are wise third parties to stimulate this. It would be especially powerful if this process could happen through mediation between the two leaders behind closed doors.

It would be difficult to go through all the lessons that we have learned. In *Holy War, Holy Peace,* I present a series of cultural de-escalation measures, well beyond the examples I have given here.[12] I argue that both sides should be encouraged to take these practical measures so that they can arrive at a different cultural space and a different moment of opportunity. Once the sides have gone through this first step, the other stages—the rational processes of de-escalation—might prove successful.

I have emphasized some cultural de-escalation measures like mourning, shared study, and symbolic shared deeds. Among those righteous deeds are visiting the sick, caring for the land, helping the poor. All of these things have to be bilateral. These acts are part of a slow and steady process that should precede and accompany any other formal negotiation. There should never again be another Oslo that is just about building industrial parks and making sure that there are adequate police forces. The latter stands for a waste of history and a waste of human lives. Instead, there should be a process that includes weekly gestures and projects of cultural change, social change, and psychological change. These changes should include influential leaders. Only then will there be a possibility of uprooting Hamas and the most brutal behavior by the military actors on both sides.

Only if we understand the intricacies of culture and symbols as well as the power of the ethical deed will we be able to withstand the pressures for destruction. Those pressures for destruction are concentrated in places like Jerusalem or the Temple Mount. I believe we are beginning to discover the central importance of ethics and culture, the centrality of honor, humiliation, and the devastating effects of cheapening human life through random violence. Nevertheless we need to go through a cultural revolution for some of these answers to begin working in our favor.

Those people who see themselves as outside the conflict have to reframe their own perceptions and the way they can intervene. All of us should recognize the importance of religious symbols, cultural institutions, and the emotional side of human existence, and also the transformative power of ethical deeds. More importantly, we should understand the power that people have to change their hearts in a way that yields practical programs of safety, security, and restoration of lost honor. This is the place in which religious values and symbols can play a pivotal role in creating or restoring national homelands that are not built on the misery of others.

NOTES

1. See Marc Ross, *The Management of Conflict: Interpretations and Interests in Comparative Perspective* (New Haven, Conn., and London: Yale University Press, 1993). Also see Kevin Avruch, *Culture and Conflict Resolution* (Washington, D.C.: United States Institute of Peace, 1998); and Kevin Avruch, Peter Black, and Joseph Scimecca, eds., *Conflict Resolution: Cross-Cultural Perspectives* (Connecticut and London: Praeger, 1991).

2. See William Ury, *The Third Way* (New York and London: Penguin Books, 2000), who has a more subtle and impressive message in recent writings. The classics in this field include Roger Fisher and William Ury, *Getting to Yes: Negotiating an Agreement without Giving In* (New York and London: Penguin Books, 1981); Roger Fisher and Scott Brown, *Getting Together: Building a Relationship that Gets to Yes* (Boston: Houghton Mifflin, 1988); and Roger Fisher, ed., *International Conflict and Behavioral Science* (New York: Basic Books, 1964).

3. See Vamik Volkan, *The Need to Have Enemies and Allies* (New Jersey and London: Jason Aronson, 1988); and Vamik Volkan, *Blood Lines: From Ethnic Pride to Ethnic Terrorism* (New York: Farrar, Straus and Giroux, 1997).

4. See R. Scott Appleby, *The Ambivalence of the Sacred* (New York and Oxford: Rowman and Littlefield Pubs., 2000); Marc Gopin, *Between Eden and Armageddon: The Future of World Religions, Violence, and Peacemaking* (New York and Oxford: Oxford University Press, 2000).

5. See Exod. 23:4 and 20:13.

6. See Deut. 20:1–17.

7. *The Works of Bernard of Clairvaux* (Kalamazoo, Mich.: Cistercian Fathers Series, 1977).

8. Mohammed Atta, translated letter available at http://www.fpp.co.uk/online/01/11/WTC_Atta_Letter.html.

9. Marc Ross, "Psychocultural and Psychodynamic Interpretations: Identity and Ethnic Politics," *Political Psychology* 22 (2001): 157–78.

10. See John Paul Lederach, *Preparing for Peace: Conflict Transformation across Cultures* (Syracuse: Syracuse University Press, 1995); and John Paul Lederach and Cynthia Sampson, *From the Ground Up: Mennonite Contributions to International Peacebuilding* (Oxford and New York: Oxford University Press, 2000).

11. For example, there are certain methods of dialogue through provocation of confrontation that I cannot support. I have seen this method in several places and it always seems to do more harm than good. It also becomes quite manipulative of raw emotions. Constructive conflict engagement is essential and should be managed wisely but not manipulated for methodological purposes.

12. Marc Gopin, *Holy War, Holy Peace: How Religion Can Bring Peace to the Middle East* (Oxford and New York: Oxford University Press, 2002).

Nuclearization in the South Asian Region: Interactions between Pakistan and India

GERALD JAMES LARSON

INTRODUCTION

It is of course important to focus on how India and Pakistan will be interacting now that both countries have demonstrated and publicly proclaimed their nuclear weapons capabilities. I wish to suggest, however, that it may be equally or more important to focus on interactions between political and military communities within each country separately. I also wish to suggest that it is important to understand some of the basic reasons for nuclearization in Pakistan and India which are interestingly different in each context. Finally, I want to comment on the role of religion as promise and peril in regard to the many geopolitical problems in the South Asian region, not only in terms of Islamic and Hindu traditions but also in terms of the academic study of religion in general. My essay, therefore, has three distinct parts: (1) India and Pakistan: The Partition Mindset and the Discourse Mindset; (2) India and Pakistan: The Reasons for Nuclearization; and (3) India and Pakistan: The Role of Religion.

INDIA AND PAKISTAN: THE PARTITION MINDSET AND THE DISCOURSE MINDSET

Let me begin with two historical narratives, the first from seventeenth-century India and the second from present-day Pakistan.

Dara Shikoh and Aurangzeb

August 29 was intensely hot in Delhi. The small female elephant on which he rode was covered with dust. He was himself dressed in filthy coarse cloth with a stained and torn turban loosely tied on his head. His fourteen-year-old son sat next to him holding tightly to his arm. Both father and son sat quietly in the howdah as the elephant walked slowly through the streets of Delhi with Nazar Beg, the slave-soldier, watching from behind with his sword drawn. As they passed through the streets of Delhi, people would give a cursory glance at the pathetic sight and then quickly turn their eyes away. They were deeply saddened by the spectacle because the man on the elephant was known and beloved by them, but they did not dare to show any emotion.

The little procession finally arrived at the prison, and father and son were taken to their cell. The heat was even more cloying inside the thick walls of the prison. They barely slept that night, their bodies dripping with perspiration, and through the next day there was little change in the foul-smelling air. The young boy wept quietly, but the father made no sound as he stared blankly at the barren floor of the cell. Then, towards evening, father and son heard some shouting in the streets outside, and suddenly there was the rush of footsteps in the hall outside the cell. The door was unlocked and Nazar Beg with two other guards came into the cell. The young boy, terrified, hugged his father. Nazar Beg pulled the boy away from his father, raised his sword, and plunged it into the father. Nazar Beg and the other guards then proceeded to hack the body to pieces.

The year was 1659. The man's name was Dara Shikoh, prince of the realm, the oldest son of Shah Jahan whom everyone had thought would be the successor to Shah Jahan. Not only had he lost the battle for succession at Samugarh, he had dared to relate Islamic theology and practice to the larger Hindu environment in which Mughal hegemony functioned. He had actually studied Hindu ideas, learned some Sanskrit, studied with a Hindu holy man, and written about the manner in which Hindu and Muslim ideas could be harmonized. His brother, Aurangzeb, and the Muslim legal specialists, the ulama, had been deeply offended by what they considered to be his heretical tendencies.

But there were to be still greater indignities, even beyond Dara Shikoh's death. By order of Aurangzeb, the pieces of Dara Shikoh's corpse were paraded through the streets of Delhi on a small female elephant and entombed in a vault under the dome of the tomb of Humayun, while Dara Shikoh's head was delivered in a box to the imprisoned Shah Jahan. Not long afterwards, two other brothers, Shuja and Murad, were also eliminated (the former by an overdose of drugs, the latter by a planned murder). Aurangzeb's triumph was complete. Of the four brothers, only he, Aurangzeb, survived.[1]

Fate was hardly kinder to Aurangzeb himself nearly half a century later. Jadunath Sarkar comments:

> The last years of Aurangzib's life were unspeakably gloomy. In the political sphere he found that his lifelong endeavour to govern India justly and strongly had ended in anarchy and disruption throughout the empire. A sense of unutterable loneliness haunted the heart of Aurangzib in his old age.[2]

For over twenty years he had pursued his Deccan conquests while the empire overall underwent inexorable decay and decline in wealth and spirit. Personal tragedy surrounded his life on all sides. It was as if the ghosts of his father and three brothers were wreaking a terrible vengeance. In his last letter, he complained:

> Old age has arrived and weakness has grown strong; strength has left my limbs. I came alone and am going away alone. I know not who I am and what I have been doing. . . .
>
> I brought nothing with me into the world, and am carrying away with me the fruits of my sins. I know not what punishment will fall on me. Though I have strong hopes of His grace and kindness, yet in view of my acts, anxiety does not leave me.[3]

Finally, on a Friday morning early in 1707, while reciting the Muslim Confession of Faith (the Kalimah or Shahada), he breathed his last. He was buried in the Deccan near Daulatabad, far from the splendor and majesty of the Mughal courts in Delhi or Agra.

Pervez Hoodbhoy and the General

In 1999, Pervez Hoodbhoy, Professor of High Energy and Nuclear Physics at Quaid-e-Azam University of Islamabad, Pakistan, received a summons from the office of the chairman of the joint chiefs of the military of Pakistan to appear for interrogation. He had been writing a number of articles against Pakistan's policy of nuclearization, and he was, thus, suspected of disloyalty to his country. Professor Hood-bhoy was questioned for a full two hours, but it became obvious as the interview unfolded that Professor Hoodbhoy was a patriot. He simply disagreed with his government's policy regarding nuclear weapons.

Near the conclusion of the interview, Professor Hoodbhoy in-quired: "General, may I ask you a question?" "Certainly," replied the General. "Under what circumstances would Pakistan use nuclear weapons against India?" The General replied: "That's an easy question to answer. If India crosses the international border [note: the "inter-national border," not the "line of control" in Kashmir] and occupies any cities of Pakistan, we will use nuclear weapons against India! Wouldn't you agree?" Professor Hoodbhoy replied: "Of course, no! If India were to occupy Pakistani cities and territory, resistance on the ground and international pressure would be so great that India could not possibly hold the territory for more than a few months, but if Pakistan were to respond to India's invasion with a nuclear attack of, say, five bombs at selected Indian cities, India would probably respond with ten or more nuclear bombs against Pakistan." The General held up his hands and asked: "How many would be killed in a nuclear attack?" Professor Hoodbhoy responded: "Perhaps 7 or 8 million people." The General then asked: "What is the population of Pakistan?" Hoodbhoy replied: "About 145 million." "See," said the General, pounding the desk with his fist, "Pakistan will never be defeated by India!"[4]

The Same Story

Nearly 350 years separate these two stories, and yet I want to suggest that they are in many ways the same. Both illustrate a clear di-chotomy between what I am calling a Partition Mindset and a Discourse Mindset. Akbar S. Ahmed has put the matter in the following way:

> From the late seventeenth century onwards Muslims faced two choices: they could either firmly re-draw the boundaries of Islam around themselves, shutting out the emerging realities, or allow the boundaries to become elastic and porous thereby effecting synthesis with non-Muslim groups. The two alternatives delin-eated were clear: legal, orthodox formality on the one hand and eclectic, syncretic informality on the other. It is no accident that these two clearly delineated and mutually opposed choices emerged in the person and character of the sons of the emperor Shah

Jahan, Aurangzeb and Dara Shikoh. No such dramatically extreme and opposed positions in the sons of the rulers of Delhi are recorded in earlier Muslim history. One of the two would succeed Shah Jahan to rule India and thereby influence the course of future history, casting shadows [even] on contemporary events in South Asia.[5]

The "contemporary events" mentioned, of course, include the debate over a "two nations" theory, the Partition of India and Pakistan, the division of Punjab and Bengal, the tragedy of Kashmir, and what Arundhati Roy has called "the end of imagination" in both India and Pakistan. They also refer to the recent nuclear testing, beginning with the May 11 explosions in the Pokharan desert of Rajasthan and continuing into Kargil and the current volatility in both India and Pakistan.[6]

J. F. Richards has made a similar observation:

During the first half of Shah Jahan's reign a long-standing political and intellectual conflict in the Mughal empire polarized around the two most able and forceful Mughal princes. The liberal party found an articulate and influential spokesman in the eldest son of Shah Jahan. Prince Dara Shikoh attracted those nobles, imperial officers, scholars, intellectuals, and others who remained committed to Akbar's eclectic ideology and policies. The conservative party found its champion in Shah Jahan's third son. Aurangzeb drew to him Muslim nobles, officers, theologians, official ulema who wished to shift the empire toward a more properly Muslim state in conformity with the Sharia.[7]

The issue here is not to praise or to blame the "liberal" or "conservative" side but simply to suggest that there always have been a Discourse and a Partition Mindset among Muslims in India, and that they carry down to the present day, so that Dara Shikoh is to Aurangzeb as Pervez Hoodbhoy is to the Pakistani general.

The dichotomy continues from the seventeenth through the twentieth century. The Partition Mindset is represented by Shah Jahan and Aurangzeb, Shah Wali-Ullah (1703–1762), Sayyid Ahmad Khan, Muhammad Iqbal, and, of course, Muhammad 'Ali Jinnah. The Discourse Mindset is exemplified by the great emperor Akbar, his great-grandson Dara Shikoh, the Deoband School of reformers, and such distinguished figures of the twentieth century as Maulana Abul Kalam Azad.

Precisely the same two mindsets are deeply embedded in Hindu or Indic (Hindu-Buddhist and Jain) traditions all the way back to Mughal times. Aurangzeb's desperate incursions into the Deccan for over two decades were frequently frustrated and undercut by the quintessential proponents of the Partition Mindset on the Indic side, namely, Shivaji, Shambuji, and Shahu, the great champions of the Marathas who refused to be assimilated into the Mughal scheme of things. On the other hand, the eclectic ideology and Discourse Mindset of Akbar or Dara Shikoh would not have been possible without the Rajput Hindu chieftains and kings who helped the great Mughal rulers to fashion the Perso-Arabic-cum-Rajput-Hindu cultural synthesis that created the unique and world-historical civilization known as the Indo-Islamic.[8]

Just as the Discourse and Partition Mindsets can be traced in Muslim social reality from the seventeenth to the twentieth century, so too can they be clearly traced in the Hindu or Indic traditions through the same period. So the Muslim League has its counterpart in the Hindu Mahasabha. Shah Wali-Ullah finds his match in later times in a Dayananda Sarasvati, and even more so, in the "Hindutva" ideology of a V. D. Savarkar, the work of the RSS (the Rashtriya Svayam Sevak), the VHP (the Vishva Hindu Parishad) and the current BJP (Bharatiya Janata Party) government in Delhi. The famous Hindu Mahasabha speech of Savarkar in 1937 could have been given by Jinnah:

> India cannot be assumed today to be a unitarian and homogeneous nation, but on the contrary there are two nations in the main; the Hindus and the Muslims. . . . There are two antagonistic nations living side by side in India.[9]

The Discourse Mindset, of course, was primarily that of the Congress Party in the early years up to Nehru, the proponents of India as a modern secular nation-state, the Ramakrishna-Vivekananda tradition, and perhaps most of all, Gandhi, who commented with no ambiguity whatever: "Partition means a patent untruth. My whole soul rebels against the idea that Hinduism and Islam represent two antagonistic cultures and doctrines."[10]

The most important question in South Asia today is not the question of the interaction between Islam and Hinduism or even between Pakistan and India, important as those issues are. Rather, it is the manner in which the Islamic traditions within Pakistan and the Hindu or Indic traditions within India will work out the two mindsets within their respective communities. The larger question of the interaction between the Islamic and Hindu civilizations will largely depend on the manner in which these issues will first be worked through within the respective communities.

INDIA AND PAKISTAN:
THE REASONS FOR NUCLEARIZATION

Nuclearization of the region, of course, has greatly increased the stakes in the long historical struggle between the adherents of a Partition and a Discourse Mindset. From the time of Partition in 1947, the Partition Mindset has tended to overpower the Discourse Mindset again and again. For the most part, the Partition Mindset has been vigorously pressed by Pakistan based upon its ideological claim that the justification for its very existence is to provide a homeland for the Muslims of South Asia. This is, of course, the primary argument for its claim that Kashmir with its Muslim majority population must eventually become part of Pakistan. This argument was severely undercut with the dismemberment of Pakistan in 1971 and the emergence of Bangladesh as an independent nation state founded largely on ethnic and linguistic rather than religious grounds. Nevertheless, Pakistan continues to maintain a Partition Mindset along with the basic claim of providing a homeland for Muslims in South Asia as a primary reason for its existence.

India, at least in the early decades under Nehru, tended to favor a Discourse Mindset based upon its basic ideological commitment to a secular, democratic state. As a Muslim majority area, therefore, Kashmir has always been important symbolic evidence of India's *bona fides* as a secular state in which a great variety of communities can have a meaningful place. As I have argued elsewhere, however, India's understanding of the notions of "secular" and "democratic" was largely Neo-Hindu, even in the early years of independence. As V. P. Singh has bluntly stated: "What has been established in the past half century is the upper caste Hindu raj."[11] This has become considerably clearer in more recent years with the emergence of the powerful political voices of the BJP, the VHP, and the RSS in the Indian polity. In other words, as has been the case since the seventeenth century, the Partition and the Discourse Mindsets are alive and well in both Muslim and Hindu contexts, with the Partition Mindset being the dominant influence time and again.

Moreover, the members of the nuclear club (Britain, China, France, Russia, and the United States) have encouraged the Partition Mindset, either through policies of benign neglect which time and again have marginalized the South Asian region, or through policies of sanctions against both India and Pakistan. Sanctions, of course, have been largely lifted since September 11, and the United States has become the third nuclear player in the region since the introduction of American military forces from October 7 onwards. Moreover, if the United Nations Monitoring Group on Afghanistan is correct in reporting that the forces of al Qaeda have access to nuclear devices as well as missiles with a range between 45 and 190 miles, there are currently four nuclear players in the South Asian region.[12] Former President Bill Clinton's comment back in 2000 that South Asia is "the most dangerous place on earth" has almost become an understatement.[13]

Be that as it may, let me turn now to some of the important reasons that led India and Pakistan to become openly declared nuclear powers. India had a nuclear energy program even before independence, and Nehru had authorized a Department of Atomic Energy (DAE) already in 1948 under the guidance of nuclear physicist Homi Bhabha.[14] India's nuclear program had always been for peaceful energy purposes, however, and Nehru in the early years was clearly against the development of nuclear weapons. The situation changed after the conflict with China in 1962, when India was badly beaten on the battlefield. Thereafter there was increasing pressure in government circles for developing a nuclear deterrent policy, especially after China successfully detonated its first nuclear device in 1964.

Following the 1971 war between India and Pakistan which issued in the dismemberment of East Pakistan from West Pakistan and the establishment of Bangladesh as an independent state, pressure grew even stronger for India to develop nuclear capability. When the United States "tilted" towards Pakistan during that conflict, and when it became clear that the United States was actively pursuing a new diplomatic rapprochement with China (with Pakistan's assistance), India under Indira Gandhi's leadership moved closer to the Soviet Union. Within a short time (1974), India detonated its first underground nuclear device. At that time, however, Indira Gandhi did not pursue nuclear weapons, arguing instead that the detonation was simply a "peaceful nuclear explosion" for the sake of developing nuclear technology.

During the same period, Pakistan also started pursuing a nuclear strategy, reaching a level of capability comparable to India's by 1979.[15] Thereafter it was widely known throughout the world that both India and Pakistan had the capacity to develop nuclear weapons, but neither country pursued nuclear matters further, at least openly, for the next two decades. All of that changed dramatically in May of 1998 when India detonated some five nuclear devices on May 11 and May 13, followed by Pakistan detonating six nuclear devices on May 28 and May 30.

There were, of course, many complex considerations for the decisions in India and Pakistan to become openly declared nuclear powers. The end of the Cold War, the collapse of the Soviet Union, the seemingly endless cross-border tensions between India and Pakistan over Kashmir, the growing influence of China in the Indo-Tibetan region, the emergence of militant Islam, and the rise of conservative Hindu ideology were all important considerations. I am inclined to suggest, however, that three reasons are especially salient for understanding the shift to open nuclearization: (1) nuclear deterrence or nuclear shield; (2) psychological anguish; and (3) the quest for stability. Let me comment about each, showing how it functions in Pakistan and India and how it appears to be having a backfire or what Chalmers Johnson has called a "blowback" effect.[16]

(1) *Nuclear shield.* Pakistan seems prepared to use nuclear weapons on a first-use strategy if Pakistani territory is occupied by India. This is already clear from my story above of Pervez Hoodbhoy and the Pakistani general. The rationale for a first-use strategy has been articulated by General Asad Durrani, former director of the infamous ISI (Inter-Services Intelligence agency):

> If we were to make it clear that whatever nuclear deterrence we might have is primarily meant to deter the use of nuclear weapons from the other side, then by so saying we will fail to deter a conventional attack. . . . [Therefore, the other side must be led to believe that] we are primed, almost desperate to use our nuclear capabilities when our national objectives are threatened, [as] for example, a major crackdown on [the] freedom movement in Kashmir. . . .[17]

Pakistan President Pervez Musharraf has recently confirmed a willingness to pursue a first-use strategy. In the April 5 issue of *Der Spiegel* in Germany, President Musharraf has told India "to count on the fact that if the pressure on Pakistan becomes too great, then nuclear weapon use (is possible) as a last means of defence."[18] Pakistan's nuclear arsenal (possibly as many as twenty to forty nuclear weapons) is under the sole control of the military, which makes a first-use strategy especially dangerous; the usual safeguards that civilian command and control procedures provide are absent.[19]

India, on the other hand, has a no-first-use policy and is committed to a minimal deterrence strategy, and its current nuclear arsenal (possibly as many as 40 to 90 nuclear weapons) is under careful civilian control.[20] This sounds innocuous enough until one reads the discussion of what this means by Gurmeet Kanwal, senior fellow of the Institute for Defense Studies and Analysis, New Delhi: India must be able to target eight to ten major urban centers in China and/or Pakistan in order to have a credible no-first-strike retaliation strategy—in other words, it must be able to inflict sufficient damage in order to deter the adversary. Given what planners call a CEP, circular error probability, it is necessary to launch four warheads at each urban center to insure unacceptable damage—hence, altogether some 40 missiles. Furthermore, to allow for possible interception and to allow for what has been destroyed in the initial attack, India must be able to launch 70 to 80 warheads. Finally, to allow for unforeseen eventualities, a prudent total minimum capacity would be approximately 150 warheads. In addition, Kanwal continues, there should be an appropriate reserve group of missiles. Says Kanwal:

> Hence, the requirement works out to 200 nuclear warheads for a minimum deterrence doctrine with a no-first-use strategy if 10 major population and industrial centres are to be attacked in a retaliatory strike to achieve a 70 to 80 percent assurance level of destruction.[21]

Kanwal concludes his analysis by pointing out that such a minimal deterrence policy requires a triad force of land, air, and sea delivery systems at an approximate cost of 47,000 crores of rupees (roughly 5 billion dollars).

The close proximity of the two nations and the possibilities of technological error or misperception make the metaphor of "shield" much less apt than the metaphor of a dark storm cloud hanging over the region. Moreover, the nuclear shield notion has apparently encouraged rather than discouraged endless cross-border conventional warfare and terrorist activity between Pakistan and India, as happened, for example, during the Kargil conflict in 1999. As Ganguly has commented: "For the forseeable future then, the overt nuclearization of the region may have contributed to nuclear security on the subcontinent while increasing the likelihood of lower-level engagements."[22]

(2) *Psychological anguish.* Pervez Hoodbhoy has expressed this reason with respect to Pakistan as follows:

> Over the years, Pakistanis have developed a collective feeling of gloom and pessimism about the future of the country as they see the continuous deterioration of governance and the inability of the state to deliver on its promises. . . . The psychological anguish must somehow be made bearable. Enter the bomb. . . . It is important to understand the extraordinary sense of desperation felt by most Pakistanis as they reel before the rapacity of political and economic elites, and see concern for the common good evaporate. Citizens have become cynical and increasingly disappointed at their historical fate, resulting in a collective loss of confidence in the state. The bomb provides the masses a refuge from reality and an antidote to collective depression.[23]

The economic and political situation in India is a good deal better than in Pakistan, but both countries suffer from massive poverty and social deprivation. Yet there was widespread rejoicing and dancing in the streets when the successful nuclear tests were announced in Pakistan and India in May 1998. One might not accept Hoodbhoy's description of the reaction as a "refuge from reality and an antidote to collective depression," but the rejoicing in the streets in both India and Pakistan was at least symptomatic of an awakened national pride. People in both Pakistan and India have long-standing feelings of inferiority and resentment against what is perceived to be the arrogance of the established nuclear powers, and the successful nuclear tests clearly alleviated some of those anguished feelings.

The Human Development Index of the United Nations ranks Pakistan at about 140th out of some 200 nations. India ranks at around 120th. The United Nations World Summit for Social Development in Copenhagen in 1995 defined "absolute destitution" using five criteria:

inadequate food, inadequate access to water, inadequate housing, inadequate access to medical care, and no recourse through education or work to undo these conditions. Over 1.3 billion of the world's human beings suffer from "absolute destitution," according to the Summit findings, and the great majority of these are in Africa and South Asia.[24] Ian Talbot, in his book *India and Pakistan*, makes the following telling observation regarding the usual "two nations" perspective on South Asia:

> The subcontinent is very much two nations, but not the two nations of Muslim and Hindu imagining. . . . Rather . . . there is the relatively economically privileged nation above, in which there is intra-elite conflict for resources in the name of caste, religion and region; and there is the nation below through which runs a common denominator of dispossession, disinheritance, poverty and marginalization. The growing economic, social and ecological struggles of the nation below (minorities, women, . . . dalits) may ultimately, like a "prairie fire" spread a new "pro-people" sense of identity which transcends existing elite styles.[25]

Nuclearization thus currently serves as a "refuge from reality and an antidote to collective depression" and as a reawakening of national pride. One can only hope that it might also result some day in a "blow-back" in the South Asian region, leading the masses to demand a different kind of answer to the region's problems than the elitist Partition Mindsets of the past.

(3) *The quest for stability*. Clearly both Pakistan and India assumed that becoming openly declared nuclear powers would stabilize the political situation in South Asia. Ganguly has expressed the argument as follows:

> Indian and Pakistani decision-makers . . . have argued that the likelihood of full-scale war in the region is now highly unlikely specifically because of the emergence of a crude form of nuclear deterrence. They contend that if nuclear deterrence preserved the peace between the two adversarial blocs during the Cold War, a similar strategic arrangement can also emerge in South Asia.[26]

The irony regarding this reason, of course, is complete. Since May of 1998, the Kargil episode has led to direct military confrontation between Pakistan and India. On October 12, 1999, the Nawaz Sharif government in Pakistan was overthrown by a military coup led by

Pervez Musharraf, the Pakistani general in charge of the Kargil incursion into the Kashmir region. On the very next day, October 13, 1999, Atal Bihari Vajpayee finally consolidated a coalition government in India known as the New Democratic Alliance made up of twenty-four political parties, led by Vajpayee's own right-wing Hindu Bharatiya Janata Party (the BJP) but propped up by an array of regional parties with a wide range of ideological views. The political balance in both Pakistan and India is exceedingly delicate, and either government could fall on any day.

Moreover, since October 7, 2001, American military power has been introduced into the region. Since December 13, 2001, as a result of the attack by Islamist militants against the Indian Parliament in New Delhi, a massive military mobilization of some nine hundred thousand troops has taken place along the international border between Pakistan and India. To make matters even worse, some fifty-eight Hindu pilgrims on a train were burned to death by an angry mob of Muslims in Godhra in the state of Gujarat on February 27, 2002. Since then over nine hundred Muslims have been killed in retaliation by Hindu mobs in various parts of Gujarat.

This is not to suggest that all of these subsequent events can be traced to the nuclearization of the region in May of 1998, but it is to suggest that the quest-for-stability political reason for nuclearization was clearly wrong-headed by any measure. Rather than stabilizing the region politically, it has made the region vulnerable to an incredible array of military conflicts, and the region is on the threshold of yet another major war, one with potentially catastrophic implications. Varun Sahni has put the matter bluntly:

> The country that launches a nuclear first strike would also suffer enormous destruction and environmental ruin, even in the unlikely event that the other side did not respond. Indian nuclear strikes against Pakistan would bring lethal clouds of radioactive fallout across northern India and cause widespread environmental contamination. If a nuclear attack by one side were reciprocated by the other, as appears likely, the entire subcontinent could become a radioactive wasteland.[27]

Very quickly, of course, such a nuclear disaster would stretch far beyond the South Asian region, with possibly devastating long-term damage to the global environment.

INDIA AND PAKISTAN: THE ROLE OF RELIGION

When I began to think about this volume's theme, "Promise and Peril: The Paradox of Religion as Resource and Threat," I found myself recalling an essay that many of us were avidly reading back in the 1960s, namely, Karl Marx's "Contribution to the Critique of Hegel's Philosophy of Right," first published in 1844, the year in which Marx also published the *Economic and Philosophical Manuscripts*.[28] These were the so-called early "humanist" writings of the young Marx. He was still under the strong influence of Hegel's and Feuerbach's notion of "alienation" (*Entfremdung*) and had not yet moved to his later intense focus on economic theorizing.

I am inclined to think that many of those comments of the young Marx are still relevant to understanding the role of religion both in regard to India and Pakistan and in general.

Marx's opening comments have, of course, become famous:

> For Germany the criticism of religion is in the main complete, and criticism of religion is the premise of all criticism. . . .
>
> Religious distress is at the same time the expression of real distress and the protest against real distress. Religion is the sigh of the oppressed creature, the heart of a heartless world, just as it is the spirit of a spiritless situation. It is the opium of the people. . . .
>
> The abolition of religion as the illusory happiness of the people is required for their real happiness. The demand to give up the illusions about its condition is the demand to give up a condition which needs illusions. . . .
>
> Thus the criticism of heaven turns into the criticism of the earth, the criticism of religion turns into the criticism of right and the criticism of theology into the criticism of politics. . . .[29]

The thrust of Marx's analysis in the essay is that there had been a long internal critique of religion (primarily Christianity) in Germany, beginning with Luther and the Reformation and coming down through the work of Hegel and Feuerbach. This critique had finally unmasked institutional religion as a "reversed world consciousness" that often veils the economic and social deprivations of ordinary worldly existence. In this regard Marx was largely following Feuerbach. In *The Essence of Christianity*, Feuerbach had argued that the religious consciousness is often an "alienated" (*Entfremdung*) consciousness in which human beings have projected predicates such as justice and love onto their awareness of God. These predicates really describe what the human condition should be, or, in other words, theology is really a form of disguised or esoteric anthropology.[30] It is only when one is able to criticize this "reversed world consciousness" that one can begin to raise questions regarding the social reality of human existence as such (the *Gattungs-begriff* or "species-notion," that is, the human being as a social being). In this sense, "the criticism of religion is the premise of all criticism." In other words, the internal criticism of religion is the beginning of all critical social science. Marx wryly notes that this criticism of religion in Germany had been primarily theoretical and that Germany had a long way to go in order to accomplish a genuine social revolution of the material conditions of German life. Still, the internal criticism of religion was "in the main complete" in Germany and the way had, thus, been opened for radical social criticism and the possibility of human emancipation.

Marx's sociological reductionism and economic theorizing have, of course, long been discredited. However, his insight, following Hegel and Feuerbach, that "criticism of religion is the premise of all criticism" is important in understanding the role of religion and the study of religion in contemporary social reality because it calls attention to aspects of religious awareness that are often symptomatic of profound psychological, political, and social dysfunctions in human understanding. Marx was himself overly prone to dismiss religious awareness as "false consciousness." But one need not accept the reductionist program in order to benefit from the notion that a hermeneutic of suspicion regarding religious discourse can be helpful in analyzing certain psychological, political, and social problems.

In this regard, I want to offer a few brief observations which I have found illuminating, and not a little puzzling. To paraphrase the opening phrase of Marx's famous first sentence, "For contemporary Pakistan and India, and the Middle East generally, the criticism of religion is *not* in the main complete." Indeed, it has hardly begun. Current Islamic discourse, whether it be in Pakistan or in any Islamic republic or in any of the contexts in which Islam is a major social presence, and whether it be right-wing, left-wing, or Islamist militant discourse, lacks any criticism of Muhammad or the Qur'an or the Shari'ah and often contains a mindless rhetoric of defeatism and external blame. In many Islamic contexts, to criticize Muhammad or to criticize the Qur'an is to commit blasphemy and to run the risk of imprisonment or even death. There are, of course, many differences and antagonisms within Islam, and there are long traditions of heretical discord that can be traced through the centuries. For the most part, however, there is little or no public space in contemporary Islamic social reality for the critical appraisal of Islam itself as a way of life. Older traditions of Islamic modernism have almost completely disappeared or have been forced underground. The Partition Mindset, in other words, has become especially prominent in recent years, and moderate voices like those of Pervez Hoodbhoy are being increasingly silenced. Khaled Abou El Fadl has commented as follows:

> Despotic and exploitative regimes have taken power in nearly every Muslim country. Most important, however, a dogmatic, puritanical and ethically oblivious form of Islam has predominated since the 1970s. . . .
>
> This puritanical theology responds to the feelings of powerlessness and defeat with uncompromising symbolic displays of power, not only against non-Muslims but also against Muslim women. . . . This contemporary orientation is anchored in profound feelings of defeatism, alienation, frustration and arrogance. . . .
>
> Islamic intellectuals have busied themselves with the task of "defending Islam" by rampant apologetics. This produced a culture that eschews self-critical and introspective insight and embraces projection of blame and a fantasy-like level of confidence and arrogance.[31]

The situation in India is not much better. There was a long tradition of the internal criticism of Hindu religion in the nineteenth century and the first half of the twentieth century that issued in the Gandhian-Nehruvian secular state. The state was Neo-Hindu to be sure, but nevertheless sensitive and responsive to the social and economic inequities that had been covered over by centuries of Hindu rationalization. The past decade, however, has witnessed the resurgence of a Partition Mindset of "Hindutva" (Hindu-ness) that is anti-secular, aggressively anti-Muslim, and increasingly anti-Christian as well.[32] As already mentioned, the Partition Mindset of "Hindutva" has been a component in Hindu sensibility throughout the modern period, and one can only hope that more moderate voices reemerge by way of recapturing the promising Discourse Mindset of a Gandhi or Nehru.

In the United States, meanwhile, a certain kind of Partition Mindset dominated public discourse from the time of Clinton's presidency until September 11, 2001. The United States turned inward domestically. Coverage of international news and foreign policy was greatly reduced. There was a preoccupation with stories such as the Monica Lewinsky scandal, the huge controversy around the manner in which chads should be counted on Florida ballots, and finally the national fascination with Gary Condit's role in the tragic disappearance of Chandra Levy.

September 11 forced the United States to turn outward and thus made obvious the paucity of American critical understanding of the crisis in West Asia, Central Asia, and South Asia at the time of the tragedy. There was a general bewilderment, from the White House on down, about why Americans should be so hated. To be sure, there had been the glowing encomiums regarding globalization in such books as Thomas Friedman's *The Lexus and the Olive Tree* and the promise of a "new world order" under the guidance of American economic sophistication.[33] Few understood, however, the role that the United States had played in maintaining the status quo among repressive regimes throughout Asia, thereby thwarting social and political change throughout most of the Islamic world.

Since September 11, there have begun to emerge, finally, a variety of sophisticated articles and books by such figures as Ahmed Rashid, Bernard Lewis, Paul Kennedy, Paul Bracken, et al. Also, Andrew Sullivan's "This Is a Religious War" in the *New York Times Magazine* (October 7, 2001), and Salman Rushdie's "This Is About Islam" in the *New York Times* (November 2, 2001) have been incipient attempts to articulate a critical perspective regarding the role of religion throughout the Islamic world and especially in Central and South Asia.

Could nuclearization, the war on terrorism, and the Partition Mindset all be related? And might the key for understanding that relation be a critical assessment of our respective religious visions? Could a Discourse Mindset link all of these visions together in a meaningful conversation, and, more importantly, in a meaningful global praxis? Could such a praxis begin to meet the needs of the absolutely destitute among us and thus bring us to the threshold of realizing our authentic

Gattungs-wesen (our "species being")? I am inclined to think that the answer to these questions is affirmative, and that the young Marx still has some relevance for those of us who engage in the academic study of religion today.

CONCLUSION

But let me return to South Asia, my point of departure. Akbar S. Ahmed has commented as follows:

> South Asia is at the crossroads, at a critical point in its history. The future looks bright but uncertain. There are more people living in middle-class comfort and more people suffering from poverty and deprivation than ever in history.
>
> South Asians must stop demonizing each other. Muslims must cease to think of Hindus as degraded kafirs to be subdued on the battlefield in a final showdown; similarly Hindus must stop thinking of Muslims as alien military invaders, unclean foreigners, to be finally defeated like the mythological Ravana. . . .
>
> A radical reassessment of recent South Asian history is required. On the threshold of the new millennium will the future bring conflict or consensus, harmony or hatred?[34]

And let me close with two verses from the famous poem of Faiz Ahmad Faiz, "Freedom's Morning—August 1947":

> This pitted dawn, snake-bitten sky of morning!
> We waited for this day. It came at last.
> But this was not our hope of heaven's dawning—
> The dreams our comrades cherished in the past.
> Hope against hope, we looked towards the sky
> To see where stars might set; that endless chain
> Of waves that lap the shore by night, then die;
> A haven for our ship; the end of pain. . . .
>
> I hear the plans we made are now complete.
> Light and dark are joined with wandering feet.
> And those who suffered quickly changed their ways;
> They celebrate the victory they achieved;
> They tell us there will be far better days.
> But they forget the pulsing heart that grieved.

The lamp upon the road is almost spent;
The morning breeze still passes with a sigh.
We know not whence it came or where it went;
And there is conflict with the heart and eye.

There may be no relief, but still we strive
To keep our cause, our cherished goal alive.[35]

The sentiment in the poem could have been uttered by any number of Muslims or Hindus over the past five hundred years—Dara Shikoh, Aurangzeb, Sayyid Ahmad Khan, Savarkar, Gandhi, Nehru, Atal Bihari Vajpayee, Pervez Musharraf—all have understood the "pulsing heart that grieved." But all could also say: "There may be no relief, but still we strive to keep our cause, our cherished goal alive."

Neither Muslim nor Hindu tradition is monolithic in practice. Both are rich and complex traditions with many voices and with a completely open-ended future. There will always be voices for Partition as well as for Discourse and Dialogue. The "cherished goals" are surely freedom and dignity and hope and the chance to live side by side in peace. Unlike the great Mughals who could only survive by killing off all rivals—even their own sons and daughters—perhaps the people of South Asia can find a better way in the years to come in the new millennium. If they fail, the consequences will be far worse than the carnage of the Mughal wars or even the devastation of Partition.

NOTES

1. The account of Dara Shikoh's death and the triumph of Aurangzeb is presented in great detail in Jadunath Sarkar, *History of Aurangzib*, 4 vols. (Calcutta: Sarkar and Sons, 1912). A shorter version is Jadunath Sarkar, *A Short History of Aurangzib* (Calcutta: M.C. Sarkar, 1962). There is also the eyewitness account of the death of Dara Shikoh as set forth in the diaries of Niccolao Manucci, in *Mogul India 1653–1708 or Storia do Mogor*, trans. William Irvine, 4 vols. (1907–1909; reprint ed., Delhi: Atlantic Pubs., 1989), 1:259–341.

2. Sarkar, *Short History of Aurangzib*, p. 359.

3. Ibid., p. 364.

4. This story was told by Pervez Hoodbhoy at a lecture sponsored by the Institute for Advanced Study entitled "Crying Wolf: Nuclear War on the

Indian Subcontinent," February 28, 2000, at Indiana University in Bloomington, Indiana. The details of the story were later confirmed in a personal conversation with Professor Hoodbhoy. I have provided the direct quotations which, in my judgment, are a fair representation of how Professor Hoodbhoy himself characterized the conversation in his lecture. There is no written text of the lecture, however, and the quotations in the story, therefore, represent a reconstruction and not a verbatim report.

5. Akbar S. Ahmed, *Discovering Islam: Making Sense of Muslim History and Society* (London and New York: Routledge and Kegan Paul, 1988), p. 79.

6. A convenient reprint of Arundhati Roy's "The End of Imagination" may be found in *New Nukes: India, Pakistan and Global Nuclear Disarmament,* ed. P. Bidwai and A. Vanaik (New York: Olive Branch Press, 2000), pp. xix–xxix.

7. John F. Richards, *The Mughal Empire*, The New Cambridge History of India 1.5 (Cambridge: Cambridge University Press, 1993), p. 253.

8. For a brief overview of Indian history in the Indo-Islamic and Indo-British periods, see Gerald J. Larson, *India's Agony over Religion* (Albany: State University of New York Press, 1995), pp. 103–41.

9. Ibid., p. 188.

10. Cited in D. E. Smith, *India as a Secular State* (Princeton, N.J.: Princeton University Press, 1963), pp. 148–49.

11. See Larson, *India's Agony*, pp. 191ff. For the quote of V. P. Singh from *India Today*, see p. 178.

12. Reported by the Associated Press, 21 January 2002.

13. Former President Clinton as quoted in Barry Bearak, "The Mystery of Chittisinghpora," *New York Times Magazine,* 31 December 2000, pp. 26–55, cited by Sumit Ganguly, *Conflict Unending: India-Pakistan Tensions since 1947* (New York: Columbia University Press; Washington, D.C.: Woodrow Wilson Center Press, 2001), p. 1 and p. 11 (note 2).

14. The definitive discussion of the history of India's nuclear development is to be found in George Perkovich, *India's Nuclear Bomb: The Impact of Global Proliferation* (Berkeley: University of California Press, 1999). A more succinct or summary treatment of the same story may be found in Ganguly, *Conflict Unending*, pp. 100–113. See also David Cortright and A. Mattoo, eds., *India and the Bomb: Public Opinion and Nuclear Options* (Notre Dame, Ind.: University of Notre Dame Press, 1996), and P. Bidwai and A. Vanaik, eds., *New Nukes: India, Pakistan and Global Nuclear Disarmament* (New York: Olive Branch Press, 2000).

15. For a brief account of Pakistan's development of nuclear capacity, see Ganguly, *Conflict Unending*, pp. 105–8. See also S. Ahmed and David Cortright, eds., *Pakistan and the Bomb* (Notre Dame, Ind.: University of Notre Dame Press, 1998).

16. Chalmers Johnson, *Blowback* (New York: Henry Holt and Co., 2000).

17. Quoted in Ahmed and Cortright, eds., *Pakistan and the Bomb*, p. 71.

18. Quoted in Shishir Gupta, "Fusion Focus," *India Today*, 22 April 2002, p. 23.

19. For the best detailed estimates of the nuclear capacity, including the number of weapons available in Pakistan and India, as of 1999, see Neil Jacob, *Repairing the Regime*, chap. 9, "Nuclear Relations in South Asia" (www.ceip.org./programs/npp/RegimeSouthAsia.htm).

20. Ibid.

21. Gurmeet Kanwal, "A Nuclear Force Structure for India," *The Statesman*, 6 January 2001, p. 6.

22. Ganguly, *Conflict Unending*, p. 110.

23. Pervez Hoodbhoy, "Pakistan's Nuclear Future," in *Pakistan and the Bomb*, ed. Ahmed and Cortright, pp. 72–73.

24. For a discussion of the World Summit, see James Gilligan, *Violence: Reflections on a National Epidemic* (New York: Vintage Books, 1996), pp. 287–88.

25. Ian Talbot, *India and Pakistan* (London: Arnold of the Hodder Headline Group; New York: Oxford University Press, 2000), p. 286.

26. Ganguly, *Conflict Unending*, p. 108.

27. Varun Sahni, "Going Nuclear: Establishing an Overt Nuclear Weapons Capability," in *India and the Bomb*, ed. Cortright and Mattoo, p. 102.

28. Karl Marx, "Contribution to the Critique of Hegel's Philosophy of Right," in *Marx and Engels on Religion*, ed. Reinhold Niebuhr (New York: Schocken Books, 1964; reprint of the 1957 edition published by The Foreign Languages Publishing House, Moscow), pp. 41–58. A slightly different translation of the same piece may be found in Karl Marx, *Early Writings*, ed. and trans. T. B. Bottomore (New York: McGraw Hill Book Co., 1963), pp. 43–59. The original German article, "Zur Kritik der Hegelschen Rechtsphilosophie," appeared in *Franzosische Jahrbucher* (1844). *The Economic and Philosophical Manuscripts* also appear in the Bottomore edition just cited, pp. 63–219.

29. Marx, "Contribution to the Critique," in *Marx and Engels on Religion*, ed. Niebuhr, pp. 41–42.

30. Ludwig Feuerbach, *The Essence of Christianity*, trans. George Eliot (Buffalo, N.Y.: Prometheus Books, 1989). The original German edition, *Das Wesen des Christenthums*, was first published in 1841 and was translated into English by George Eliot in 1854. George Eliot, of course, was a pseudonym for the English novelist and freethinker Mary Anne Evans. The most important study of Feuerbach's thought is Marx W. Wartofsky, *Feuerbach* (Cambridge: University Press, 1977); see especially chap. 8, "The Philosophical Context of Feuerbach's Critique of Religion," pp. 196–251.

31. Khaled Abou El Fadl, "What Became of Tolerance in Islam?" *Los Angeles Times,* 14 September 2001.

32. For a discussion of the various religious crises in contemporary India, see Larson, *India's Agony,* pp. 226–77.

33. Thomas Friedman, *The Lexus and the Olive Tree* (New York: Farrar Strauss and Giroux, 1999).

34. Akbar S. Ahmed, *Jinnah, Pakistan, and Islamic Identity* (London and New York: Routledge and Kegan Paul, 1997), pp. 246, 253, 251.

35. Faiz Ahmad Faiz, "Freedom's Morning—August 1947," in *An Anthology of Urdu Verse in English,* trans. David Matthews (Delhi: Oxford University Press, 1995), pp. 68–71. Reprinted by permission of Oxford University Press India, New Delhi.

State-Religion Partnership:
Boon or Curse?

BHIKHU PAREKH

In 1996 the U.S. Congress passed the Personal Responsibility and Work Opportunity Reconciliation Act. Among other things, this act permitted faith- and community-based organizations to compete on equal terms with secular organizations for government contracts to provide day care, refugee settlement, assistance for the homeless, crisis intervention, substance abuse treatment, and other social services. The law was part of a general overhaul of the structure of welfare services, and was intended to reassure faith-based organizations that the government valued their role and saw them as partners. During its four years of existence, the law was largely ignored by the federal administrators, most of whom were hostile to its aims.

Determined to overcome their resistance, the incoming president George W. Bush issued an executive order on 29 January 2001, called "Rallying the Armies of Compassion."[1] The order reiterated the role of faith-based organizations in combating crime, removing poverty, and strengthening families. To allay fears of excessive religious entanglement and bias, it insisted that the government should follow the "principles of pluralism, non-discrimination, endowments, and neutrality" in awarding contracts. The order created Centers for Faith-based and Community Initiatives in five cabinet departments, namely, Health and Human Services, Housing and Urban Development, Education, Labor, and Justice. Each center was asked to conduct a department-wide audit of the barriers to partnership between government and faith-based organizations. Their initial findings suggested that the federal government showed a systematic bias against faith-based organizations. Some of them were prevented from applying for government funds, and were required to give guarantees that they would remove or cover up religious art and symbols and even drop references to God in their mission statements.

In the Congress and the country at large, views on the subject remain deeply divided. Some remain committed to the Jeffersonian "wall of separation" and consider state-religion partnership a retrograde and highly dangerous step. Others argue that the "wall of separation" has neither a constitutional nor a historical basis, and is largely a product of the narrowly neutralist liberalism that influenced the decisions of the Supreme Court from the 1950s to the 1980s and which the Court itself has in recent years begun to modify. In their view religion has a valuable public role and the state should find appropriate ways of forging a partnership with it.

In Britain, as in most other European countries, close association between state and religion has long been a part of political life and does not arouse the kind of resistance and hostility it does in the United States. In recent years, however, the relation between state and religion has become a subject of agonized public debate. England has an established church. While some defend this as a worthwhile and benign expression of the country's history and national identity, others think that it privileges Protestant Christianity and discriminates against people of other religions or none. Britain also has a long tradition of publicly funding religious schools. There are 6,384 primary schools of this kind (out of a total of 25,000) educating just over a third of the children, and 589 secondary schools educating around 17 percent of the children. The overwhelming number of them are Christian (including one Greek Orthodox and one Seventh-Day Adventist), the rest Jewish (32), Muslim (4), and Sikh (2). About 57 percent of these schools teach religious education according to their own beliefs, and the rest teach a multifaith syllabus. The Labour Government plans to expand their number on the grounds that there is a great public demand for them and that they produce better academic results and have a distinct mission and ethos. Critics argue that their advantages are greatly exaggerated and outweighed by their disadvantages, such as that they are divisive, open to the danger of fundamentalism, and likely to foster hatred of other religions, and that they stand in the way of developing common citizenship. They want the government to phase out the existing religious schools rather than increasing their number.

In their own different ways, the current debates in the United States and Britain have raised in a new form the old question of what the relation between the state and religion should be. In this paper I discuss this question and suggest how best we might answer it. The answer would obviously vary from society to society, depending on the value it places on religion and individual liberties, its religious homogeneity, degree of secularization, cultural traditions, and history. For analytical convenience, I shall confine my discussion to liberal societies, which share broad moral and political principles and provide a conceptually coherent framework.

WHY PARTNERSHIP?

We can readily agree on two things. First, since the liberal state is committed to basic individual liberties, especially the liberty of religious belief and conscience, and to the equal treatment of its citizens, it should not impose, institutionalize, endorse, or identify itself with religion. It must not make religious belief a precondition of citizenship or base its laws and policies on religious considerations. If it did any of these, it would directly or indirectly require its citizens to subscribe to a particular religion, and it would thus violate their freedom of conscience and liberty to hold different or no religious beliefs. In addition, it would privilege some groups of citizens or at least discriminate against others, and thus treat them unequally.

Second, since religious and secular activities overlap, state and religion cannot be neatly separated. Religious beliefs and practices have social consequences, and the state has a legitimate interest in the latter. This is why even liberal states regulate religious activities on grounds of public order, health, morality, and social harmony, and discourage religious beliefs that incite rebellion against it or hatred and violence against other religions. Furthermore, because religious individuals and groups make religiously based secular demands on the state, it cannot ignore religion altogether. This is why the state rightly grants exemption from military service to those opposed to it on conscientious grounds, allows religious oaths in courts or at swearing-in ceremonies of government officials, exempts Seventh-Day Adventists from working on Saturdays, and makes provision for the religiously based dietary requirements of those serving in the armed forces. No state, however secular (France) or committed to the wall of separation (the United States) dares to ignore these demands on the ground that it takes no cognizance of private religious beliefs.

The state, then, should be neither identified with nor indifferent to religion. Its primary concerns are secular, and center on such matters as public order, public morality, territorial integrity, and public well-being. The otherworldly destiny of the human being and the well-being of the human soul fall outside its purview. However, where religious beliefs and practices impinge on secular matters, they are of legitimate interest to the state, and it deals with them in terms of secular considerations. On this there is a broad consensus among liberal thinkers and societies. The questions that have now emerged on the public agenda are rather different. They concern whether the state and religious groups should cooperate on substantive issues. Should the state allow religious groups to assume some of its public functions, support them when they do so, allow them to compete with secular organizations for government tenders? If so, how can it do this consistently with its basic commitment to individual liberties and equality? Since liberalism has traditionally been concerned to separate state and religion and to protect each against the other, it has taken little interest in and has little to say on the nature and extent of their positive cooperation. Not surprisingly, liberals are uncertain or ambiguous in their answers.

Many of the problems facing modern societies are too complex and intractable to be tackled by individuals acting alone. They call for collective action, and the state has a vital role. It has its limits, however. Its methods are too crude and bureaucratic to cope with the diversity of situations; its administrative and moral reach is limited; and, if it is invested with too many functions and too much power, it threatens individual liberty and initiative. There is much to be said for organized action by voluntary organizations. However, they might not spring up in areas where they are most needed, lack adequate resources, do not last long enough to make an impact, or suffer from lack of coordination. There is therefore a strong case for a partnership between them and the state, the latter assisting them, devolving some of its functions to them, coordinating their activities, and working with them without turning them into its bureaucratic arm. It is hardly surprising that such state-civil society partnership is becoming increasingly popular in all liberal societies.

Voluntary organizations are of different kinds, some religious, others secular. There is no obvious reason why the state should eschew cooperation with the former. The state aims to provide certain services, and all that should matter to it is whether the organizations concerned have the capacity to provide them in conformity with officially prescribed norms. If they have, then to bar them from competing with the rest for government resources is to subject them to unfair discrimination.

Sometimes religious organizations have unique strengths which give them an edge over their secular counterparts. Many of them have long historical experience of running charities and providing welfare and other services. Since religion matters deeply to many people, religious groups also have a great motivational power. They are able to inspire their followers to give generously of their time and energy, and can be highly economical to run. At their best, they also have the capacity to build close personal relations with their clients, reconcile individuals and communities, heal wounds, nurture self-esteem, and put together broken and despondent selves. Such strengths make them particularly helpful in dealing with such matters as premarital pregnancy, juvenile delinquency, rehabilitation of prisoners and drug addicts, and gang warfare, in all of which state bureaucracy is generally too blunt to be effective.

An analysis of the various projects and services run by the Church of England in Britain found that they gave their beneficiaries a strong sense of self-esteem and empowerment, involved them as active participants in tackling their problems, were particularly good at bringing out the best in them, provided customized and noncondescending services, were prepared to take calculated risks, and were often innovative in their approaches.[2] Not surprisingly, the reoffending rate among their clients was much lower than in equivalent state-run programs. This was also the case with the Interchange Freedom Initiative founded in Texas in 1997. Its partly secular, partly religious program consisted of a strict regime of prayer, scripture reading, job training, and family counseling, and it was particularly designed to suit the kinds of prisoners involved. Just under 13 percent of the prison inmates (15 out of 120) who had gone through it went back to prison, compared to the 50 percent recidivist rate for Texas as a whole.[3] One should not generalize from such limited data, especially as they relate to religious organizations working on a wholly voluntary basis. However, they do give some indication of the potential moral resources of religious organizations. Unless there are strong reasons to the contrary, it makes little sense to waste these resources out of an uncritical deference to a narrowly defined secularism or doctrine of the wall of separation.[4]

Since religious organizations can play a valuable public role, the state should treat them equally with the nonreligious ones. They should receive tax exemption for their charitable activities as well as such other assistance and facilities that the state offers to their secular counterparts. They should also be able to compete for government tenders and receive public funds for the provision of social and welfare services. Equal treatment of religious and nonreligious organizations involves complex judgements. In some cases their religious character might count against them, as when their clientele is religiously mixed or intensely vulnerable to religious blackmail or when the services they provide are highly sensitive. In other cases it might favor them, as when the clientele belongs to the same religion or prefers a religious organization or when the services provided have a strong moral or religious element. In either case the state cooperates with them as providers of services, and either views their religious character as irrelevant or values it only because of its functional significance. The state's cooperation with religious organizations does not involve religious entanglement or compromise its secular character.

When religious organizations provide publicly funded secular services, they act as public agencies and are subject to the same general constraints as are other organizations. They must recruit and treat their staff fairly, provide proper conditions of work, establish adequate procedures for dealing with their complaints and grievances, provide services to all without discrimination, and be open to government inspection. Since they are religious in character, some of these constraints need to be relaxed, especially when they prefer some candidates to others because of their religious ethos. In appointing their senior staff, they may take account of their religious affiliation when it is essential for the delivery of services for which they are publicly funded. Although they should not proselytize, for that involves using public funds for sectarian and unauthorized purposes, they may be allowed to retain their religious symbols. To ask them to remove these is to ask them to deny their identity; it creates a situation in which no self-respecting religious organization would want to cooperate with the state. It is also unnecessary because such religious symbols can hardly be said to exert undue religious influence on their clients. The clients either never notice them or treat them as an inconsequential part of the organizational landscape and should not be presumed to be so gullible or religiously insecure as to feel pressured by the very sight of them.

I have so far discussed cases where religious organizations provide publicly funded services to all without discrimination. Sometimes they might limit their services to their own followers. In such cases they should be expected to collect and do in fact generally collect the required funds from their fellow religionists. However, they might be unsuccessful and ask for state support, raising the question whether such support should be offered. If they seek public funds for purely religious services, such as for buying copies of the scriptures, providing religious training, propagating the religion, and celebrating religious festivals, the liberal state may rightly decline on the grounds that it cannot officially endorse any form of religious activity.

The situation is different when the services in question are secular in nature, such as day care for children, centers for the elderly, hospices for the terminally ill, and counseling for those in distress. For understandable reasons, some groups of individuals might want to turn for these services to their churches, synagogues, or other religious organizations rather than to state-run institutions. It is difficult to see how the state can deny support to these organizations. The citizens concerned are asking for the same services as others, except that they would like these to be provided by an organization of their choice. And the state primarily funds the secular activities of these organizations, and takes account of their religious character only because of its particular competence in providing secular services. All that the state can legitimately require is that the services should be just as good and involve no additional cost, and that the organizations concerned meet the legal and other requirements the state imposes on all such providers.

RELIGIOUS SCHOOLS

One of the vital services provided by the state is education, and it generally does so through schools set up and sometimes administered by it. While agreeing that education up to a certain age should be compulsory, many classical liberals, including J. S. Mill, wondered if it was in the interest of individual liberty, choice, and diversity to give the state a monopoly in this area. Most liberals today have no such doubt and are convinced that the state is the best social agency of education. They allow private schools, but reluctantly and on condition that they are privately funded. Yet in many liberal societies, some groups of parents strongly prefer religious schools. And that raises the question whether they should be allowed and, more importantly, whether they should be publicly funded.

Education involves three parties: children, their parents, and the society at large as represented by the state. Their interests do not always harmonize, and we need to find the best way of reconciling them. Although children are too young to decide what is in their best interest, they can certainly indicate what schools they like or dislike and where they feel most at home. Let us assume for the sake of argument that, like their parents, they prefer religious schools. In a liberal society, these choices should be respected. However, the matter is not so simple, for choices that harm the public interest are rightly restricted or disallowed. The question then is whether religious schools harm the public interest. We might feel that they are likely to be divisive, discourage common citizenship, teach obsolete dogmas and information, and incite hatred of other religions. If these dangers are real and there is no other way of avoiding them, we may legitimately disallow religious schools and deny parents the liberty to set them up or send their children there. However, such a step is too extreme and should be avoided, especially as there is a better way of dealing with the situation. We can allow these schools on condition that they meet certain basic requirements. For example, they should teach the prescribed curriculum, not incite religious hatred, employ qualified staff, and be open to government inspection. In this way we safeguard public interest, respect parental liberties, and avoid parental protests. It is hardly surprising that all liberal societies have adopted this compromise, and that not even the most secular among them has ever thought it right or prudent to ban religious schools altogether. The question whether religious schools should be publicly funded is far more complex and has received different answers in different liberal societies. In Sweden and the Netherlands, they are fully funded by the state. In others they are partially funded by the state. In Britain, for example, the state pays their running cost and 85 percent of their capital expenditure. In the United States they receive no public funding. Each country has historical reasons for adopting its particular policies.

It is sometimes argued that if there are good reasons to allow religious schools, then the same reasons also justify their public funding. This argument is flawed because the criteria involved in each case are different. Broadly speaking, an activity should be permitted in a liberal society if it causes no harm to others individually or collectively, or if considerations of individual liberty outweigh the harm. Public funding implies, in contrast, that the state approves of the activity concerned, believes it to be in the public interest, and thinks that it should be supported by revenue raised from all citizens. It should therefore be provided only when an activity serves valuable public purposes and benefits the community as a whole. The question is whether religious schools meet this stricter criterion.

Religious schools do serve valuable public purposes.[5] First, since liberal societies value freedom of choice, they should aim as far as possible to widen the range of options available to their citizens. Religious schools are one such option. Second, religious schools have a distinct ethos, as well as distinct traditions and moral perspectives, and they help foster diversity of character, attitudes, and ways of living among their pupils. Such diversity adds to the liveliness and richness of society, avoids the domination of a single vision of the good life, nurtures different forms of excellence, and represents a valuable collective resource. Third, competition is as valuable in education as in other areas of life. Different types of schools represent different pedagogical methods, different balances between curricular and extracurricular activities, and different forms of organization, and thus help create the rich body of experiences which we need in order to make informed public judgments on different aspects of education. Fourth, for obvious reasons the state should not have a monopoly of education and exercise total control over its content. Allowing religious schools is one way of avoiding this. Fifth, education should aim not only to train the mind but also to achieve worthwhile social, moral, and spiritual goals. Some religious schools achieve all these in a way that many state schools do not. And even those religious schools that are academically below average generally have a good record of maintaining discipline; discouraging drugs, premature sex, consumerism, and bullying; encouraging social responsibility; and developing a sense of community among staff and pupils. While criticizing their spirit of dogmatism, anti-intellectualism, and conformity, we ought not ignore their virtues.

In addition to the argument based on valuable public purposes, there is also an equality-based argument for funding religious schools. The liberal state is committed to the equal treatment of its citizens. Since it funds regular schools, not to fund religious ones is to discriminate against them, as long as the education they offer is just as good, meets government criteria, and avoids additional cost. In almost all liberal societies, the state rightly provides textbooks, transport, and testing services to all children, including those attending religious schools. There is no good reason why this should not be extended to their running and construction costs as well. Contrary to what some writers have argued, religious schools do not constitute an expensive taste for which parents can be required to pay themselves. They are simply another way of providing the education the state demands of all its citizens. The religious component of education might perhaps be seen as an additional service requiring a parental contribution, as is the case in Britain. Since, however, it can be shown to be in the interest of society as a whole and not just that of the children or their parents, it would seem to deserve public support.

Public funding of religious schools carries with it certain obvious constraints. The state makes education compulsory and funds it because of the vital public interest in having well-educated citizens. Since the good life, including the life of a citizen, can be lived in several different ways, we should not take too narrow and rigid a view of good citizenship and shape all future citizens in a single mold. Such a narrow view arbitrarily delimits the range of human possibilities and is also difficult to agree upon. We should therefore insist upon those skills, attitudes, civic virtues, habits of thought, and bodies of knowledge that are necessary to enable future citizens to run their lives intelligently, live in peace and harmony with each other, earn their living, and participate in the conduct of collective affairs. The state may therefore legitimately lay down a broad curriculum that all schools should teach, a body of values and attitudes they should aim to foster, and a set of institutional rules and practices they should all observe.

Religious schools must meet these requirements if they are to deserve public funding. They should teach the basic curriculum without compromising it by such religious education as they might care to impart. They should respect and foster values that are central to any good society, especially the liberal, such as respect for fellow human beings, equality, civility, tolerance of differences, respect for the law, and peaceful resolutions of disagreements. Whatever other values and virtues they may cultivate, they must be required to cultivate these. Their employment and other practices should also meet the requirements of the law. They should employ qualified staff selected through open and fair competition, giving preference to their religious affiliation only when it is relevant to the teaching of particular subjects or maintenance of the school's ethos. They should also be publicly accountable for their teaching and use of public money, and should be open to periodic state inspection in just the same way as other schools are.

These and other requirements sometimes create difficulties for religious schools. All religions offer some account of the emergence of humankind and nature, the Christian creation story being one of them. They therefore want to teach these to their pupils. This has its obvious dangers, but we should not get them out of proportion. Even if children did not learn about, say, creationism in schools, they would learn about it in churches and at home, and there is no way to insulate them against it. They are also exposed to alternative accounts in the society at large and in the books they study in schools. We can surely depend on these to alert students to the fallacy of creationism and other such doctrines. Indeed religious schools themselves realize that if they taught untenable doctrines, they would lose their pupils' and parents' trust, make fools of themselves, and fail to attract pupils. This is one of the reasons why few of them teach them today, and why those who do feel defensive. We should not forbid the teaching of such doctrines but rather require that they also teach a more widely accepted body of scientific knowledge.

The same applies to teachings about the existence of God and even the inequality of the sexes. Almost all religions contain traditions that support an inferior status for women, and no religious school true to its history can avoid saying so. To require them not to teach or even mention it is not only an act of unacceptable censorship but also impossible to enforce. What we can and should require them to do is to teach the opposite view as well, and should rely on the rest of the curriculum, the influence of the society at large, and the pupils' own capacity to think to help them see the absurdity of the religious view. As already mentioned, religious schools well know that they forfeit their moral authority if they teach untenable doctrines. While insisting on the core values which are non-negotiable and on which there is a broad consensus in liberal societies, we should allow schools greater freedom in respect to others, and trust their good sense and self-interest, the influence of the wider culture, and the pupils' own common sense and powers of thought to steer them away from dubious values and attitudes. Deeply fearful of the potentially deleterious influence of religion and traditions, many groups of liberals are keen to use the state-sanctioned coercive and moral power of the school to shape the captive collection of future citizens in a particular mold. For reasons discussed earlier, this tendency should be resisted. While insisting on the core values necessary for any kind of good society, we should leave enough space for fostering moral and cultural diversity.

Religious schools can and do take several forms. Some are schools first and religious second, and are secular for all practical purposes. Some have religious symbols on their walls, prayers, celebrations of religious holidays, and so on, but their religious activities are largely formal, voluntary, and do not detract from the school's main task of teaching and getting good academic results. Some belong to a particular religion and have a strong religious ethos, including compulsory collective worship, periodic retreats, and moments of meditation and self-reflection, but all this has little effect on the education they provide and does not compromise their secular curriculum and aims. Some give religious education a much greater curricular space, insist on the rote learning of the scriptures, challenge secular knowledge on the basis of such doctrines as creationism, and discourage critical thought and liberal values. Such schools need to be carefully monitored lest they should violate the basic purposes of education and fail to equip their pupils with the basic values, virtues, and skills referred to earlier. If they are found inadequate, they should be denied public funding and even the right to exist. Finally, some religious schools are genuinely multireligious in their composition, ethos, and practice, respecting and teaching all major religions and providing excellent secular education. In short, like state schools, religious schools vary greatly in the ways in which they are organized and combine religious ethos with secular education. It is therefore a grave mistake to think that they are all basically the same, and equally prone to dogmatic and anti-secular education. If we fail to discriminate between them, we not only do many of them injustice but cannot even understand why thoroughly secular and even atheist parents sometimes prefer to send their children to religious schools, or why some of these schools foster strong secular values.

Public funding of religious schools does raise difficult practical questions, but these are not beyond resolution.[6] I shall take three by way of illustration. It may be asked if every religious group should be free to set up its schools. The answer is yes if its beliefs and practices are within the acceptable range, if it has institutional credentials, and if it meets the basic criteria mentioned earlier. If we think that a particular religious group is unlikely to meet them despite its assertions to the contrary, we may deny it public funding altogether, give funding on a conditional basis, or subject the school to a more rigorous regime of inspection.

It is sometimes contended that since it is not easy to find out if a religious school is encouraging fundamentalist, sexist, or racist attitudes or hatred of other religions, we should discourage all such schools. This is like saying that since some people misuse alcohol, it should be banned altogether! A well-planned inspection of the school including the texts taught and interviews with teachers and pupils can easily identify its ethos. We can also forestall or counter these dangers by requiring that all schools follow officially prescribed textbooks and that they teach and admit a certain percentage of pupils of other religions.

It is sometimes argued that religious schools ghettoize children, discourage interreligious contacts, and militate against the spirit of common citizenship. The danger is real but exaggerated and can be minimized. It does not apply to schools that are multireligious in their ethos and aims, or to those denominational schools which admit children of different religions. As for others, the danger can be minimized by such devices as twinning schools belonging to different religions and requiring them to admit a certain percentage of children from other religious communities, employing several academic and administrative staff members from different religious groups, and teaching other religions.

We are right to worry about the dangers and disadvantages of religious schools, but we should not be blind to their strengths either. Many an evangelical school in the United States and madrassas in Muslim countries offer a travesty of good education, but many Catholic,

Protestant, and even Muslim schools in Europe and elsewhere provide excellent all-round education. We also need to appreciate that religion matters much to many, and that the best way to deal with its likely pathology is to bring it into the public realm and subject it to its discipline. Determined parents will either set up private religious schools or send their children to those run by dubious organizations after normal school hours, and neither is open to public scrutiny. If teaching about religion is made an integral part of the curriculum in all schools, it might reduce the demand for separate religious schools. And existing demand is best met by publicly funding religious schools and requiring them to meet public criteria.

CONCLUSION

Whether one likes it or not, religion is an important part of people's lives, and so far the forces of secularization have not been able to eliminate its continuing influence. It has its dangers as well as strengths. Both political realism and wisdom require that the state should come to terms with it and harness its resources for the betterment of human life. I have argued that state and religion cannot and should not be either identified or totally separated. When cooperation between the two is socially beneficial and feasible, and when it can be achieved without violating basic individual liberties and equality or compromising the secular character of the state, it should be welcomed. We should build, not an impenetrable wall of separation between them, but a fence of demarcation. The fence both separates and relates them, respects their distinct identities, promotes common interests, and provides a shared and friendly neighborhood of separate households.

NOTES

I am most grateful to my good friend Leroy Rouner for many long discussions on this subject, and to Larry Cahoone for his helpful critical comments.

1. "Rallying the Armies of Compassion," White House, 29 January 2001. The irony of the title could not have been lost even on the President. See also "Unlevel Playing Field," White House, August 2001.

2. Paul Lawless et al., "Community-based Initiative and State Urban Policy: The Church Urban Fund," *Regional Studies* 32 (1998).

3. "With Help from a Hidden Hand," *The Economist* 10 (February 2000).

4. For a useful discussion, see Mary Jo Bane et al., eds., *Who Will Provide? The Changing Role of Religion in American Social Welfare* (Boulder, Colo.: Westview Press, 2000).

5. For a good analysis, see Martha Minnow, *Washington Post,* 24 February 2002.

6. For a valuable discussion of the arguments for and against religious schools, see the various articles in *Oxford Review of Education* 27, no. 4 (2001). The whole issue is devoted to this subject.

PART II

Religion in Itself

Awe as Promise and Peril: The Entheogenic Evidence

HUSTON SMITH

An essay whose title contains the word *peril* is likely to be heavy going, so I shall begin with a touch of whimsy. My recent book on this essay's subject, *Cleansing the Doors of Perception: The Religious Significance of Entheogenic Plants and Chemicals*, happened to be reviewed in my local newspaper two weeks before Christmas, and it carried the caption "Angels We Have Heard While High." That was so inspired that if there were a Pulitzer Prize for headlines, I would have nominated it for that year's award.

Turning now to my subject: under the umbrella title for this year's volume—Religion as Promise and Peril—I have chosen to focus on the subject of awe. I shall be using the word *entheogens* (a word I shall soon define) as my case study for exploring this subject, but before turning to those substances I want to speak to the phenomenon of awe per se.

AWE

The first thing I want to say about it is that we have, for the most part, lost it. With its central heating, painkillers, and improved medical care generally, technology has now cushioned us from nature's raw and wild side and may have played a part in this loss. Whatever the reasons, we do not experience awe as readily as our ancestors did. Moreover, we don't clearly understand what awe is and how central it is to religion when religion is vital. We've domesticated our religion. Churches tell us that God loves us, which happens to be true, and urge us to do good works, which we certainly should, but those are not the be-all and end-all of religion.

So what is awe?

It is the central and distinctive religious emotion. It fills these criteria by uniting two emotions that elsewhere are opposites—fear and fascination. Fascination draws us toward its object while fear holds us back. Fascination arises because, the veil having been rent, one sees new, momentous vistas that one had theretofore not known existed. That's gripping—one thinks of Moses seeing Mount Sinai in flames. But fear accompanies this fascination, for one does not know if the new domain is habitable. Are the natives friendly, so to speak? Saint Paul, who, Anselm said, understood Moses better than he (Anselm) could, tells the Hebrews in his letter to them that "so terrifying was that sight that Moses said, 'I tremble with fear'" (Heb. 12:21). Seven verses later, Paul draws the implications for the Christian church: "We offer to God an acceptable worship with reverence and awe, for indeed our God is a consuming fire." Having himself been struck blind on the Damascus Road, Saul, thereafter Paul, knew what awe is.

Prior to the entheogens, I hadn't known. Having had a Christian upbringing that took, I had read the Bible every day of my adult life without noticing how prominently fear figures in it. It's everywhere. "Worship the Lord in holy splendor; *tremble* before him all the earth" (Ps. 96:9). "Work out your salvation with *fear* and *trembling*" (Phil. 2:12). "It is an *awful* thing to fall into the hands of the living God" (Heb. 10:31). Christian liturgy is likewise studded with references to God's awe-filled-ness: "God's "*dread* Judgment Seat," the "*terrible* mysteries" of the eucharist table, and the God we "*dare* to call Father." On the Hellenic side of Western civilization, Plato tells us in his Allegory of the Cave that the prisoner who is released from the cave will at first find the outdoor light so *painful* to his eyes that he will have to turn away from it. And when Plato refers to his own epiphanies, he says that "first a *shudder* runs through me, and then the old awe creeps over me."[1] In India we have the blood-curdling eleventh chapter of the Bhagavad-Gita in which Arjuna, having begged to be shown Krishna's cosmic form, withdraws his request when he finds how terrifying that form is. "Deep is my delight [that's the fascination part] but my *dread* is greater."[2] Gordon Wasson draws all this together by saying that awe "is not fun. Your very soul is seized and shaken until it tingles. Who would choose to feel undiluted awe, or to float through that door yonder into the Divine Presence?"[3]

That dread requires further comment, for as the above citations have probably strongly suggested, it is not ordinary fear. If a tiger were to charge us we would be afraid, as we would be if a lunatic were to step from the wings and start spraying us with bullets. But those are ordinary fears because they are understandable. The fear in awe—awe-filled fear, to resort to the original meaning of the word *awful*—is of a different species. It is provoked by something that belongs to a different order of being whose workings we cannot understand. If, in place of the lunatic or tiger, a ghost were to stare at us intently as if it were looking for someone, we would experience a very different kind of fear. Halloween plays on this difference, as do ghost stories and horror novels generally. Words that connote this second, eerie kind of fear are *spooky* and *dread*. Confronted with something uncanny, we stand aghast, or find ourselves shuddering. Chills run up and down our spines, our hair stands on end, and our scalps tingle. I have not been able to track down the story in Jewish lore that when a profane person dared to enter the holy of holies in the Jerusalem temple that was reserved for the High Priest, he emerged with the horse's hoof imprinted on his forehead.

ENTHEOGENS

Let us now turn to the entheogens which I am using as my case study for the phenomenon of awe. *Entheogen* is a neologism so I should begin by defining it. Coined by Carl Ruck, the word denotes a small class of nonaddictive plants and chemicals that can occasion mystical experiences. Etymologically, the root of the word carries connotations of God-containing—as when the Native Americans refer to peyote as God's flesh—or God-enabling. The popular word for these substances continues to be psychedelics, but the "psychedelic sixties" built such strong connotations of recreational use into the word that people who want to approach them seriously (as candidates for scientific research) and reverentially (as potential catalysts for religious renewal) find it important to give them a name that points upward. Denotatively, the best known of the substances I am referring to are mescaline, psilocybin, LSD, and the newcomer from Brazil, ayahuasca, but anthropologists have found comparable substances in innumerable tribes all over the world.

I chose the entheogens for my case study on awe because it was through them that I discovered what awe really is. When it happened, the discovery that I hadn't actually known awe came as a shock, for I

mess and who hope that entheogenic experiences will straighten them out should especially be warned against using them except in psychiatric settings.

5. *Spiritual harm.* Here I include thinking that having mystical visions proves that one is authentically religious and even enlightened, with the spiritual arrogance this can breed. The test of authentic religion is reduction of egocentricity and increase in empathy for others. As the useful adage has it, the test is altered traits, not altered states—altered traits of conduct, not altered states of consciousness. A subset of spiritual harm is unwise life-course deviations—being knocked off an otherwise sane life trajectory. Timothy Leary was especially guilty of perpetrating this danger with his siren call to rebellious youths in the 1960s to "tune in, turn on, and drop out."

6. Finally, *reductionism.* Reductionism is a standing threat to religion, because it refuses to take religious claims at face value and it demotes them to epiphenomena. Generated by what? Candidates range from wishful thinking (Marx), to stunted psychological development (Freud), or, as the latest version of this fallacy, neurotheology, contends, specifiable brain patterns. (A recent cover story in a news magazine carries the caption, "God in the Brain.") To counter reductionism, Aldous Huxley once admonished me that in speaking of the entheogens I should never say they *caused* religious experiences but should always say they *occasioned* them.

Because reductionism has been perhaps the major ploy by which our secular society has forced religion to the sidelines of intellectual and public life, it is worthwhile to strike at its roots and point out that it presupposes a metaphysical view of the mind and that this view of the mind is arbitrary because metaphysical systems can never be proven to be true. According to the contractual view of modernity, the mind is a generator, whereas philosophers from William James to C. D. Broad and biologists of the stature of Henri Bergson believe that it makes equal if not more sense to think of the brain as a reducing valve. In Broad's words, "the function of the brain and nervous system and sense organs is in the main *eliminative* and not productive. Each person is at each moment capable of remembering all that has ever happened to him and of perceiving everything that is happening everywhere in the universe. The function of the brain and nervous system is to protect us from being overwhelmed and confused by this mass of largely useless and irrelevant knowledge."[4]

Aldous Huxley placed Broad's view at the heart of his own perennial philosophy, saying, "According to such a theory, each one of us is potentially Mind at Large. But in so far as we are animals, our business is at all costs to survive. To make biological survival possible, Mind at Large has to be funneled through the reducing value of the brain and nervous system. What comes out at the other end is a measly trickle."[5]

These perils of entheogens are real, and in some cases not negligible. On the whole, though, they are low—far lower than risks relating to nicotine and alcohol. And as with freeway driving, flying, and using fire, we have the knowledge to reduce the risks to levels that seem acceptable when they are weighed against the benefits the substances can yield. The history of the Native American Church seems to stand as incontrovertible proof of this.

As a transition to the promising side of the ledger, let me remark in passing that these substances appear not to be for everybody. People seem to divide instinctively and impulsively according to whether they are drawn to or repulsed by them. Mircea Eliade seems to have been a good example of the second class. When a former student of his, Robert Forte, asked to interview him on the subject, Eliade kept putting him off until Forte said he seemed to be nervous about the subject, to which Eliade replied, "No, yes, no—well, I just don't like those things." Gordon Wasson and his wife wrote a history of civilization—*Mushrooms, Russia, and History*—in which the whole human story hinges on the division between the half of the world that has loved mushrooms and the other half that has found them repulsive, calling them toadstools and the like. I will not go into whether the division is geographical, as the Wassons thought, or between personality types that crop up everywhere—the "set" of ingestors as defined above. The division itself, though, seems to be real.

I turn now to the promise of the entheogens, specifically their religious promise. Other possible contributions—such as those that excite psychiatrists, mental health professionals generally, and brain researchers—will not be taken up here.

ENTHEOGENIC PROMISES

The promise of the entheogens is twofold. First, they might improve our knowledge of religious history—including, for believers, our understanding of how God works in the world. Second, they might restore the religious worldview to its rightful place in our individual and collective lives.

Beginning with the first of these possible benefits, it has now become quite clear that consciousness-changing substances have woven in and out of religion from as far back as we can see. Soma, peyote, and the *kykeon* of the Eleusinian mysteries are the best-known examples; and a swami of the Ramakrishna Vivekananda Order who was in the audience when this lecture was delivered orally sent me a follow-up note telling me that there is a reference in Patanjali's *Yoga Aphorisms* to *ausadhi* ("herbs") that aid yogic practice. More interesting is the possibility that such substances figured in the great epiphanies—revelations—that launched the great historical religions. Mary Barnard broached this possibility in 1963 in an essay that appeared in *The American Scholar* titled "The God in the Flowerpot." She asked there,

> Which was more likely to happen first, the spontaneously generated idea of an afterlife in which the disembodied soul, liberated from the restrictions of time and space, experiences eternal bliss, or the accidental discovery of hallucinogenic plants that give a sense of euphoria, dislocate the center of consciousness, and distort time and space, making them balloon outward in greatly expanded vistas?[6]

Her answer is that

> the latter experience might have had an almost explosive effect on the largely dormant minds of men, causing them to think of things that they had never thought of before. This, if you like, is direct revelation. Looking at the matter coldly, unintoxicated and unentranced, I am willing to prophesy that fifty theobotanists working for fifty years would make the current theories concerning the origins of much mythology and theology as out-of-date as pre-Copernican astronomy.[7]

In the years that have followed that prophecy, evidence has come to light that strengthens it. Raymond Prince, a medical anthropologist, has pointed out that the brain states produced by entheogens are close to ones that result from physical exhaustion and the delirium that attends certain infectious diseases. He concludes from this that in the long stretch of human history, far more visionary experiences came by way of the latter two causes than from entheogenic plants that are hard to come by. One thinks of the austerities that preceded Buddha's enlightenment, Moses' forty days on Mount Sinai—where was the food and water?—and Jesus' temptation visions in the course of his forty days in the wilderness. Of course, the danger here is that reduction-ists will seize upon this reading of history as support for their con-tention that visions are epiphenomenal only. But since they cannot even explain how brain states give rise to ordinary thoughts and feel-ings, they have no business pontificating about epiphanies.

The ultimate promise of entheogens, though, is that they might revitalize religion and regain for it the respect it deserves in our public intellectual life. How so? Because, after the light of the great out-of-doors has been directly *seen*, it is never again possible to take the shadows on our cave's wall as final reality. Up until the rise of modern science, every culture and civilization took it for granted that the every-day world our physical senses report is presided over by a nobler world that created it—circling the globe from east to west there was the Dreaming of the Australian Aborigines, East Asia's Heaven, South Asia's Nirvana, the Abrahamic religions' Yahweh, God, and Allah, and the Hellenic Agent Intellect and the One. If science had discovered a single fact that disproved the existence of this Greater World, we would have to content ourselves with its worldview. As it hasn't, it makes per-fect sense to accept entheogenic theophanies as true.

CODA

I will end on a personal note.

For the opening epigraph in my *Cleansing the Doors of Percep-tion* I quote Aldous Huxley as saying that "the mescaline experience is without any question the most extraordinary and significant experi-ence available to human beings this side of the Beatific Vision." In the course of preparing this lecture, however, I realized that I didn't have clearly in mind what Huxley thought the Beatific Vision has over entheogenic ones, so I reread him to find out. It falls short on two counts, I discovered. First, entheogenic visions are transient. And sec-ond, though they tip toward compassion—"some of the compassion and some of the gratitude remains after the experience is over," Hux-ley attests—compassion is not solidly and centrally built into them.

Huxley believed with Pascal that "truth without charity is not God, but his idol," and with Meister Eckhart that "what is taken in by contemplation must be given out in love." Hence, he wrote, "I am not so foolish as to equate what happens under the influence of mescaline or of any other drug, prepared or in the future preparable, with the realization of the end and ultimate purpose of human life: Enlightenment, the Beatific Vision. All I am suggesting is that the mescaline experience is what Catholic theologians call 'a gratuitous grace,' not necessary to salvation but potentially helpful and to be accepted thankfully, if made available."[8]

NOTES

I am indebted to Robert Forte and Robert Jesse for helping me with this essay.

1. Plato *Phaedrus* 251a.

2. Swami Prabhavananda and Christopher Isherwood, *Song of God: Bhagavad-Gita* (New York: New American Library, 1944–51), p. 96. Barbara Stoler Miller's translation reads, "I am thrilled, yet my mind trembles with fear," *The Bhagavad-Gita* (New York: Bantam Books, 1986), p. 107.

3. Gordon Wasson, quoted in "Wasson's *Soma*: A Review Article," *Journal of the American Academy of Religion* 40, no. 4 (1972): 485.

4. C. D. Broad, quoted in Aldous Huxley, *The Doors of Perception* (New York: Harper & Brothers, 1954), pp. 22–23.

5. Ibid., p. 23.

6. Mary Barnard, "The God in the Flowerpot," *The American Scholar* 32, no. 4 (Autumn 1963): 584.

7. Ibid., p. 586.

8. Huxley, *Doors of Perception*, pp. 29, 30, 34.

Killing for Salvation:
Aum Shinrikyô and the
Perils of Religion

IAN READER

INTRODUCTION

On March 20, 1995, five members of the Japanese new religion Aum Shinrikyô unleashed the nerve gas sarin on the Tokyo subway. Aum had made the sarin in its program of arms development, a program linked to what its charismatic leader Asahara Shôkô saw as Aum's cosmic mission to enact a "salvation plan" (*kyûsai keikaku*) to destroy materialism and bring about a spiritual transformation of the world.[1] The attackers did not see themselves as committing an atrocity: they were "true victors" (*shinri shôsha*) fighting to further Asahara's "salvation plan" in a final cosmic war against the outside world, which was a "den of evil" (*akugô no sôkotsu*)[2] in need of purification. They believed that their status as sacred warriors allowed them to commit such deeds as killing those who did not follow the true path of (and hence had rejected the salvation offered by) their sacred master Asahara.

The attack killed twelve people and caused consternation in Japan and beyond. It was, at the time, the most significant terrorist attack of modern times, seemingly indiscriminate and targeting a mass civilian population. Therefore March 20, 1995, is a critical date in modern Japanese history, and it had the same sort of psychological impact that September 11, 2001, has had in the United States. It undermined the confidence of a public already troubled by economic recession, destroyed Japan's cherished belief in the safety of its society, and led to an extended period of public questioning of all aspects of Japanese society and culture.[3] It also led to debates about religion, since Aum was legally registered as a religious movement under Japanese laws, enjoying legal protection and advantageous tax breaks. Prior to such registration, movements are assessed to ensure that they conform to legal stipulations that they contribute to the public good (*kôeki*). Thus, after the subway attack, questions were asked about why the authorities had awarded such a status to Aum, especially when it became clear that Aum had long been suspected of committing earlier crimes. As investigations into Aum began after March 1995, evidence emerged that Aum had been involved in several other killings, including a chemical weapons attack which killed seven people in the town of Matsumoto in July 1994; the killing of a lawyer investigating complaints against Aum who disappeared with his family in November 1989; and the murder of dissident members. Further evidence also showed that Aum had tried to develop biological, chemical, and other forms of weapons to use in its envisioned cosmic war with society at large. Asahara and leading disciples were subsequently arrested and put on trial.

AUM IN JAPANESE RELIGIOUS PERSPECTIVE

The involvement of a registered religious organization in extreme violence led to a "paradigm shift" in modern Japanese thinking. Prior to Aum, the consensus (based on Japan's prewar experiences of state suppression of religions) was that religions needed protection from the state. After Aum, it seemed as though both society and the state needed to be protected from religions. Debate also centered on whether Aum could be considered a religion at all, given its actions. In public discourse it has now generally come to be seen as a "cult" (*karuto*), a term that in Japanese popular usage implies fraud, criminality, and manipulation. Similarly, Asahara has been portrayed simply as a power-mad megalomaniac who pretended to be a religious teacher and who stole ideas from others to construct a plausible-sounding religion so as to further his criminal schemes.

The idea that Aum could not have been a "real" religion was based on the assumption that "religions" are intrinsically "good." Hence, the reasoning went, if Aum had committed evil acts, it could not be a "religion" and thus had to be something else, either a criminal group masquerading as a religion or an innately bad "cult." Ironically, the perception of religion as inherently "good" also influenced the few who defended Aum when the first allegations of criminality surfaced. On two occasions scholars (one from Japan, one from the United States) made statements exonerating Aum of crimes it was accused of, because they saw Aum as a religious movement with sincere followers. They assumed that this meant it would have been impossible for Aum devotees to commit crimes.[4]

Those who deny that Aum is a religion because of its deeds, or assume that it could not have committed crimes because of its religious nature, are left with no avenues for understanding Aum. In assuming the essential "goodness" of religion, they preclude any consideration of how a religious movement might be involved with evil acts. If one is to begin to understand what happened in Aum, and learn from it, it is essential to jettison the notion of religion as an essentially "good" entity. As suggested by the images of promise and peril, resource and threat, conveyed in this volume, religion is perhaps best considered as intrinsically value-neutral—but with a capacity for producing the best of human endeavor and, occasionally, the worst.

This perspective is borne out by an analysis of Aum, which was, after all, legally registered as a religion in Japan. To acquire that recognition, it had satisfied the authorities that it possessed attributes required of religions under Japanese law, such as an organizational structure aimed at promoting religious teachings and practices. Aum also exhibited other elements normally considered to be characteristic of religions: views of death and after-lives; practices aimed at developing the spiritual awareness of disciples; an emphasis on belonging to a community with a spiritual purpose; a leader who laid claims to spiritual authority that transcended the mundane world; conceptions of truth, good, and evil; and so on.

Moreover, Aum did not start out with a mission to kill. Rather, between its formation in 1984 and the subway attack of 1995, it underwent a dramatic shift in orientation that cannot be explained simply by portraying it as evil from the outset. Such an "interpretation" offers no way of explaining how and why such radical changes occurred or why an optimistic millennial movement became bent on destruction. Nor does it explain how and why Aum members changed from idealistic yoga practitioners aspiring to save the world into zealots who believed that everyone outside their increasingly enclosed circle was damned, and that they could justifiably kill others so as to save them. Finally, it also fails to explain how and why Asahara changed from an ascetic, strict, yet compassionate teacher of spiritual disciplines into an overweight, paranoid figure involved in sexual relationships with female disciples and obsessed with imagined conspiracies against him.

My argument is that such changes occurred because of a complex process which involved Aum's religious orientations, and therefore can only be fully understood through recognizing Aum's nature as a religious movement. Asahara's self-perception and sense of mission, his teachings, and the events Aum experienced at critical junctures in its development profoundly influenced its views of the world and impacted on its emergent doctrines. Since space does not permit an extended consideration of this process,[5] I will here focus on some major aspects of Aum's teaching and practices from its early years. These are where the seeds of violence were implanted in the movement.

AUM IN ORIGIN AND NATURE

Aum, like many late-twentieth-century new religions in Japan, was fired by the notion that the world was in crisis and the present age about to end, resulting either in world destruction or in the emergence of a new spiritual civilization. It believed that it had a crucial role to play in this process, and that its partially blind founder, Asahara Shôkô (b. 1955–), had a mission to defeat the forces of evil and to establish a spiritual realm on earth. Asahara had become interested in asceticism, yoga, meditation, and spiritual healing in the late 1970s and had initially joined Agonshû, a new religion. The founder of Agonshû, Kiriyama Seiyû, combined an emphasis on esoteric Buddhist practices with millennial teachings in which he and his movement aspired to bring about world transformation.

In 1984 Asahara's belief in his own spiritual powers and growing sense of personal mission led him to quit Agonshû and set up a yoga and meditation group in Tokyo. Its fifteen or so members became the core of his new movement. Initially the yoga and meditation group focused on ascetic practices designed to remove negative karma and to lead disciples to enlightenment. It quickly evolved into a larger religious movement in which these individual aims remained paramount, but were welded to a collective mission of salvation in which the group sought to transform the world spiritually. In this process, Asahara was transformed into a "guru" (as he was called by devotees), spiritual master, and messiah. This spiritual elevation developed after a series of revelations in 1985 and 1986 which convinced Asahara that he had been selected to carry out this mission.

Aum grew quickly because of Asahara's evident personal charisma and his ability to express his ideas in accessible terms. Many who met him in the 1980s and early 1990s found him to be a warm, kind, and spiritual man with excellent communication skills. Yet he also had another side. In describing him to me, disciples spoke of great acts of compassion and kindness, which naturally strengthened their feelings towards him—and yet stated that he could also be brutal and harsh, driving them to extremes in ascetic practice. This "compassionate cruelty," Asahara believed, was essential to his role as a guru: at times he had to be cruel and force his disciples to engage in ascetic practices, because this was necessary for their spiritual liberation. However, this cruel compassion posed dangers for the group, since it ultimately legitimated the use of force within the movement, thus setting it on the road to wider violence.

Like many new Japanese religions, Aum was eclectic in nature, drawing teachings from a variety of sources. It combined Buddhist practices designed to increase psychic power with an emphasis on the importance of karma in determining one's destiny in subsequent lives, and with its aforementioned millennial beliefs. Such ideas were reinforced by concepts assimilated from other sources: Hinduism, from which Aum drew its yoga practices and the worship of the Hindu deity Shiva, who is associated with destruction and asceticism; Christianity's Book of Revelation, whose concept of a final war between good and evil added force to Aum's millennialist views; and Tibetan Buddhism, from which Aum derived notions relating to death and transformation and to the nature and role of gurus, as well as further inspiration for its millennial views. As befits a very new movement in the early days of development, and in the first flush of charismatic excitement, its teachings were liable to rapid and sudden change as the movement and its leader encountered new challenges and questions that needed resolution.

The movement's initial name was Aum Shinsen no Kai ("Aum Hermit's Society"); in 1987 this was changed to Aum Shinrikyô ("Aum Supreme Truth"). Both names are significant for what they say about the movement's self-perception. *Aum* comes from Sanskrit, and refers to the powers of creation, preservation, and destruction inherent in the universe. In this triad, destruction (represented in the Hindu pantheon

by Shiva) signifies the power to destroy evil and hence is a force of
ultimate good. This image was central to Aum's millennialism and
reflected its view that any spiritual improvement in the world necessi-
tated the destruction of negative forces. The term "hermits" (*shinsen*)
in its first title indicates the importance Aum placed on asceticism and
withdrawal from the world for the sake of spiritual self-development,
while its use of "truth" (*shinri*) indicates its belief that it was the sole
source of ultimate truth in the world. In Aum *shinri* ("truth") referred
both to the movement and to the concept of truth. The two were syn-
onymous, so any criticism of Aum was an attack on "truth" and any
critic of Aum an enemy of the truth.

Initially, devotees focused on ascetic practices intended to eradicate negative karma, purify the body, and liberate the mind. The concept
of karma—the notion that any deed has spiritual repercussions—was
crucial to Aum. Its members believed that individuals accumulate
karma through every deed and thought on earth, and that their karma
determines their fate after death, when they would either transmigrate
to higher spiritual realms or fall into lower realms (including terrible
hells). The correct spiritual path led to liberation in this world and
hence to higher realms thereafter. However, because karma was essentially a negative force that reflected the inherent evils of the phenomenal world, the normal human fate was to accumulate negative karma
and thus fall into the hells. To avoid such a fate, Asahara believed,
humans had to withdraw from the material and corrupting world and,
under the guidance of a spiritual master, engage in ascetic practices
that would lead them along the correct path to enlightenment.

Karma was not just individual but collective: it was through the
accumulated negative karma of individuals that the world at large was
facing a crisis. Aum asserted that humanity's materialism and neglect
of spiritual endeavors had produced a collective negative karma that
had brought the world to the brink of destruction. In various prophe-
cies from the mid-1980s onwards, Asahara stated that such destruction—in the form of natural disasters, environmental pollution, and/or
nuclear war—would occur at the end of the century because of collective bad karma. Yet there was an initial optimism to his views, since
he believed that such disasters would have a purifying effect, sounding
the death knell for materialism and leading to the emergence of a new,
spiritually oriented world. Destruction, then, could have inherently
positive dimensions.

Moreover, this transition might even be accomplished without mass destruction. If, Asahara stated, Aum could produce an army of enlightened practitioners to spread its teachings across the world before the end of the century, it would be able to eradicate all negative karma, conquer materialism, and peacefully bring about a new spiritual paradise on earth. This was its salvation mission, and it was a message of optimism and idealism that attracted several enthusiastic devotees. One devotee I interviewed in 1998, for instance, testified that it was the idea of taking action to help the world in this crisis, and being one of the elite chosen to save the world, that drew him to Aum. In 1987, Aum began to accomplish this mission of collective salvation. It founded communes known as Lotus Villages, to which devotees could withdraw to concentrate on ascetic practices. And it established its sangha (using the Buddhist term for a community of devotees), a group of followers who renounced the world by severing ties with their past and with their families in order to concentrate on becoming spiritual warriors fighting for the collective salvation of humanity.

THE SEEDS OF DISASTER

Thus Aum initially exhibited a number of idealistic visions centered around individual enlightenment, asceticism, and practice, along with an optimistic belief that it was engaged in a mission of salvation through which its spiritual warriors would overcome evil and transform the world. These idealistic and optimistic visions, however, gave rise to a number of problems that facilitated the irruption of violence in Aum.

The establishment of communes and a sangha, for example, created tensions between the movement and the world at large. In attracting a number of young followers who were prepared to leave their families and join their communes, Aum acquired an inner core of extremely dedicated and zealous devotees who had no qualms about shunning their families and entering a path of extreme asceticism. Yet this gave rise to an anti-Aum movement: the families of those who had often simply abandoned university courses or jobs to join Aum filed legal complaints against the movement when they were denied access to their offspring, and eventually formed an anti-Aum opposition group. This opposition was also supported by various rural communities in the areas where Aum had acquired land for its communes, and where its stance as a radical, communal movement conflicted with the values and attitudes of its conservative rural neighbors. From 1987 on, Aum ran into repeated conflict around its communes as it found its building plans blocked by hostile authorities and as it rode roughshod over local laws to press ahead with building communes without permission.

The communes and sangha, in other words, helped develop a sense of estrangement from and conflict with the world at large. They also strengthened the introverted vision of devotees, who had no further moral or spiritual capital invested in the society they had left, and who thus were prepared to devote themselves entirely to the alternative morality Aum created. This introversion was reinforced by Aum's teachings on salvation and enlightenment, which emphasized a notion widely found in Buddhist thought: that the external world was ephemeral compared to the true reality of the interior world. As members of Aum informed me, in order to eradicate karma one had to concentrate on one's own practice, which took precedence over all else. This created a self-directed, introverted mind-set among followers, in which collective salvation was always seen as secondary to their own practice and liberation. This internalized way of thinking enabled devotees to remain unaware of what their leaders were doing, even when, in the 1990s, Aum was making weapons and preparing for actual war. Devotees I interviewed in 1997 and 1998 excused their lack of awareness of the violence their movement was committing by saying that they were too absorbed in their own practice to focus attention on the (illusory) external world. Some even made it clear to me that they felt Aum's crimes were of little relevance compared to the "real" issues they faced in their inner spiritual practice and asceticism. This introversion meant also that there were few mechanisms inside the movement to restrain the activities of its leader, once the movement began to slide into violence.

This emphasis on one's own practice, coupled with withdrawal from and incipient conflict with the wider world, gave rise to an elitism in Aum. Because they were performing ascetic acts, and because they were engaging in a mission of salvation, practitioners readily developed a sense of moral superiority over those outside the movement. This development was facilitated by the ways in which Asahara claimed the mantle of a messiah, and proclaimed his disciples as sacred warriors and true victors. Conflicts with parents and neighbors heightened this sense of elitism, "proving" to Aum devotees how unworthy and mired in delusive thinking those outside the movement were, and how spiritually superior they themselves were—a mindset that helped foster the belief that they had the "right to kill" those less spiritually advanced than themselves.

THE DEVELOPMENT OF VIOLENCE AND
THE ROLE OF THE GURU

Aum faced problems not only because of external opposition but also because of an increasing sense of millennial urgency within the movement. By 1988 Asahara was concerned that the targets and goals he had previously proclaimed as necessary means for saving humanity were too distant to be realized. Although Aum had a small number of highly dedicated ascetic practitioners, there were by no means enough to produce the sort of spiritual army needed to eradicate the world's karma by the end of the century. Hence violent rather than peaceful world transformation became an increasingly likely prospect.

In addition, Asahara had become frustrated because some disciples were less than zealous about their ascetic practices, and he felt compelled to hasten the progress of his followers by any means possible. Here he drew inspiration from esoteric Buddhism and its concepts of the guru. In various Buddhist texts, there are stories in which gurus or bodhisattvas are justified in committing acts that normally would be seen as "wrong" if their acts actually produce positive results. Thus a bodhisattva may treat others nonvirtuously in order to save them from greater karmic suffering. For example, in some Buddhist stories a bodhisattva, who was able to see the future of a man who was otherwise destined to kill 500 people in his life, interceded by killing the man. Thus the bodhisattva spared the victims and saved the potential perpetrator from the terrible karmic repercussions of such deeds.[6] In others, gurus act cruelly to force their disciples to make spiritual breakthroughs. The Tibetan story of how the guru Marpa acted harshly towards his disciple Milarepa, testing him almost beyond endurance so that he broke through to supreme enlightenment, particularly interested Asahara, who saw it as indicative of how a true guru should act.[7]

In other words, such stories and texts combined with Asahara's frustration at his disciples' lack of endeavor and his growing sense of urgency to give rise to escalating demonstrations of "compassionate cruelty" in which disciples were coerced into doing austerities or beaten if they did not. Such actions actually elevated Asahara's spiritual status by showing that he was an enlightened and compassionate teacher who was owed total obedience. One of the products (or corollaries) of Aum's turn to violence was an intensification of devotion towards Asahara, and an increase in the levels of obedience he expected followers to show. This marked a dangerous new phase in the development of the movement: violence became acceptable and legitimate when ordered by the guru, and his authority became paramount and unquestioned.

In thus going beyond normative morality, and in demonstrating his apparent spiritual powers by so doing, Asahara entered into a moral vacuum where there ultimately were no binding moral rules. Besides being permitted to use violence against his disciples, he was released from sexual constraints and earlier ascetic demands. He is not alone in this: there are many cases of guru figures whose morally reprobate behavior has become transformed, through the eyes of devotees, into expressions of sanctity and spiritual power, or who may even behave immorally in order to "prove" their spiritual prowess. For example, in her essay on the Tibetan teacher Chogyam Trungpa, whose alcoholic and sexual excesses blatantly infringed Buddhist moral codes, Sandra Bell has emphasized what Trungpa's disciples saw as his "crazy wisdom." By behaving in immoral ways, Trungpa was demonstrating that he was not bounded or restricted by convention; he was thus affirming just how spiritually advanced he was.[8] Equally, Asahara's disciples, rather than being shocked or repelled by his behavior, saw in it a validation of his status as a guru. One devotee told me that was how he expected gurus to behave since they were not bounded by the normal parameters of the world. Thus, rather than undermining his position as a holy figure, breaches of conventional morality actually enhanced it and reinforced the growing sense of moral and spiritual superiority of those associated with him.

ACCIDENTAL DEATH, CRIMINAL BEHAVIOR, AND DOCTRINAL CHANGE

In autumn 1988 a crucial turning point occurred in Aum. This was the accidental death of a devotee, Majima Terayuki, during cold-water austerities ordered by Asahara. The event created a terrible dilemma for Aum at a time when it was facing growing external opposition. Since the death occurred during austerities ordered by Asahara to advance Majima spiritually, it could lead people to challenge Asahara's abilities as a guru capable of giving true guidance, and could give rise to accusations that, despite claiming to be a messiah, he could not even save his own devotees. It is clear, too, that the incident had a grave psychological impact on Asahara, who soon afterwards became unwell and began to exhibit signs of paranoia, complaining that he was being spied on and that there were infiltrators in Aum who were seeking to undermine him.

Asahara and a small group of senior disciples immediately decided to "defend the mission" by covering up the death, incinerating the corpse, and disposing of the ashes. In Japan it is a criminal act to dispose of a corpse without proper procedure and without informing the authorities; at this point Aum entered into the realms of illegality in a way that left a dark and dangerous secret at the heart of the movement. The self-serving, defensive cover-up was designed to save the leader and his teachings. It resulted in a further turn towards violence and in a rethinking of Aum's doctrines in relation to death, the rights and duties of spiritually advanced beings, sacred conflict, and the millennium.

In seeking to understand how and why his disciple had died, Asahara rethought Aum's basic teachings about karma and death. It was central to Aum's teaching that when one died, one would be judged on one's deeds in this life and this would affect one's rebirth. However, it was within the power of the guru to help the departed attain a good rebirth through merit-transferring rituals and by interceding spiritually at death. The former notion was very similar to normative Japanese Buddhist custom, where it is standard practice for priests to perform memorial services to facilitate the passage of the deceased to other realms after death. Similar notions occur in Tibetan Buddhism, and Asahara drew on this tradition in conceptualizing Aum's views of the role of the guru in facilitating the transition to another realm. In Aum this doctrine was known as *poa* (which, in effect, meant "transformation") and it indicated the power of the guru to "transform" the spirit at death. It developed into a crucial mechanism for, and legitimation of, murder in the movement's subsequent teachings.

Majima's death led Asahara to amend the concept of *poa*. Since he had died during austerities rather than going on to attain liberation, it followed that Majima did not, at that point, have the capacity to attain spiritual liberation in this life. Thus, he *must have had to die* under the guru's guidance so as to attain a good rebirth. Indeed, dying under the tutelage of his guru actually improved his chances of a better rebirth: he had needed to be transformed through the guru's actions so as to gain salvation. Thus *poa*, which initially indicated that a guru could assist the deceased after they had died, came to mean that the living could be transformed by the guru *through* death and thereby gain spiritual merit. It also suggested that death under the guidance or at the hands of the guru could help one escape from the karmic bonds of this life and attain liberation beyond.

This hasty adaptation of doctrine was done to cover up Aum's deeds and to protect Asahara's position and status as a guru, and it was clearly a panic-stricken response to an event that threatened both the movement and the guru. In effect, Asahara was now saying that the value of his mission was greater than the life or death of a single individual. This calculated view was set forth on other occasions, too, when Aum came under threat, and was a statement of grave moral presumption in which Asahara effectively declared his movement to be above and beyond moral and civil law.

Majima's death also affected Asahara's teachings on world salvation. He was already worrying about whether he could continue with a universal salvation plan when relatively few people appeared to be listening to him. As befits a messiah with a grand sense of mission, he failed to blame himself in this and assumed that, if his mission was failing, it was because humanity at large was refusing to take heed of the opportunity for salvation he offered. Majima's death showed that he could not always save his own disciples in life. Now he began to think that he would not be able to save everyone else and to conclude that, since people were not heeding his message, perhaps they were not *worthy* of salvation. Henceforth, he would not strive to save everyone. Rather, he would abandon the world at large to its fate because it had failed to listen to his teachings and he would concentrate on his "true victors."[9]

Shortly after Majima's death, a disciple drew his attention to the Bible and the Book of Revelation, and Asahara encountered the term *Armageddon*. The images of the final war of good and evil portrayed in Revelation fit with his visions of the triumph of good over evil. They also suggested that the final war would be, not symbolic, but real; that the followers of evil would be destroyed physically; and that world transformation required real, physical destruction. He found similar messages in other texts, notably the Buddhist Kalacakra Tantra, which presents the image of a sacred Buddhist king coming forth to lead the forces of good in a final war against evil, and to create a golden age of Buddhism on earth. Such images of merited destruction advanced in other religious traditions reinforced his growing views about the need to confront his opponents, and convinced him that his mission henceforth was not just to fight against evil but also to punish the unworthy. Just as violence was being inculcated into Aum as a legitimate course of action, such texts appeared to affirm the inevitability and merits of a real war.

MURDER AND THE RIGHT TO KILL

Majima's death was a turning point, taking Aum into the world of illegality, leading it to develop explanations and justifications for the deaths it caused, and edging it along the path of confrontational millennialism. Some months later, in February 1989, it gave rise to more extreme criminal behavior. Taguchi Shûji, a disciple present at Majima's death, announced that the incident and cover-up had destroyed his faith, and that he was leaving and was going to inform the authorities of what had happened. Since Taguchi could not be dissuaded, Asahara had him killed. Asahara argued that if Taguchi were allowed to tell the authorities what had happened, it would destroy Aum, the mission of salvation would be wrecked, and there would be no chance that a better world would emerge. Such actions would have cataclysmic karmic repercussions for Taguchi: if he destroyed the salvation mission, Asahara argued, he would accumulate such bad karma that he would spend many aeons languishing in the deepest hells. Taguchi was clearly deluded in pursuing his planned course of action and thus had to be saved from himself by being "*poa*-ed" (that is, killed). Taguchi was then killed by a group of senior disciples on the instructions of Asahara, who shortly after gave a sermon in which he stated that there might be occasions when it would be necessary to "transform" (that is, *poa*/kill) someone to prevent them from committing sins that would otherwise cause them to accumulate bad karma and suffer a terrible fate after death.[10] The doctrine of *poa* thus had shifted again, from being a form of ritual service done after death to transform and purify the spirit thereafter, to becoming (with Majima) a process of transformation that enabled people to have "good" deaths, to being (with Taguchi) a process of intervening in, and terminating, someone's life in order to save them from acquiring negative karma. Cold-blooded murder thus became religiously justified as a form of "killing for salvation."

Asahara's close disciples embraced this doctrine enthusiastically. The reasons for this were not hard to discern: *poa* indicated that it was not merely the right but the duty of advanced spiritual beings to "save" sinners by terminating their lives. Killing was thus both confirmation of one's spiritual status and a means of elevating it—a point a senior disciple, Nakagawa Tomomasa, emphasized when he was chosen by Asahara for a subsequent "salvation mission." As Nakagawa confessed after his arrest in 1995, he felt pride and elation at being chosen for the task. It confirmed his place in the spiritual elite and told him he had attained high levels of spiritual transcendence where he could, like his guru, go beyond the boundaries of conventional morality and kill with impunity.

PUBLIC HUMILIATION AND THE DESCENT
INTO DESTRUCTIVE PARANOIA

Thus, in the traumatic period between 1988 and 1989 Aum had moved from internal coercion of disciples to the use of murder as a means of defending its mission. From this period until 1995, Aum's history is one of growing estrangement from and confrontation with society, as it became fixated on the sinfulness of humanity, and increasingly convinced that those who lived in this world without seeking the path of truth would be condemned to endless aeons of living in the hells after death. Hence their only salvation would be to have this life terminated as soon as possible, thereby reducing their chances of piling up further bad karma.

At the same time, Asahara became increasingly engulfed by paranoia caused both by Aum's growing conflicts with the outside world and by the stresses accrued because of the dark secrets within the movement. Such paranoia is not uncommon among enclosed, introverted, millennial movements. In advancing the view that they alone are right, they can easily come to believe that everyone else is therefore against

them and trying to do them down. This certainly was the case with
Aum, which further withdrew into communes across Japan, and further intensified its earlier policy of persuading members to sever ties
with their families, after the traumatic period following Majima's death.

From the early 1990s onwards, conflicts and disputes surrounded
Aum everywhere it turned. Suspicion that Aum might have been involved in the disappearance of a prominent opponent was voiced in
the mass media, adding strength to the campaigns of its other opponents and leading to increased paranoia in the movement. Aum saw
such criticisms as "persecution"—and persecution is, of course, a powerful mechanism for enhancing faith and confirming one's own righteousness. The belief or delusion that Aum was being persecuted in
turn enabled Asahara to understand and interpret every problem he
faced; the failure to recruit followers and to succeed in advancing
its mission thus came to be seen not as failures, nor even as due to
humanity's inability to recognize the truth. Instead, they were clearly
the products of a conspiracy aimed at stopping Aum from achieving its
mission. Failure, in other words, was the result of conspiracy and persecution—an interpretation that further affirmed Asahara's belief in
the truth of his cause.

The notions that the world was damned, that Aum alone held the
truth, and that external forces were conspiring to destroy Aum and
undermine the truth became entrenched in Asahara's thinking during
the 1990s, and especially after the most traumatic of all Aum's experiences. In February 1990, Asahara and several disciples stood in the
national elections for the Upper House of the Japanese Parliament.
While running for election might appear to be an odd course of action
for a movement that was so critical of worldly affairs, there were evident reasons behind the decision. Other new religions had in the past
successfully advanced their agendas through political engagement, and
the election offered Aum a platform through which to get its messages
across to the nation. The result, however, was a disaster: Aum's campaign was widely mocked in the press, as were Asahara's preachings
of doom, and all Aum's candidates lost heavily.

The election was the final breaking point between Aum and
society. To Asahara the election was humanity's last chance to embrace
the truth, and it had rejected it. The Japanese people were so deluded
that they had refused the chance of salvation—and hence deserved to
be punished. Not long after the election debacle, Aum first tried to

vent mass destruction on the Japanese public, in a failed attempt to release biological weapons—in this instance botulism spores—in Tokyo. Clearly—as with all Aum's crimes—vindictiveness and a desire to punish those who had offended it were primary motives in the act. Details of this first attempt at mass destruction (like the Majima and Taguchi incidents) only came to light after the police investigations into Aum in 1995. However, it is now clear that after February 1990 the notion of mass destruction became fixed in Asahara's mind as a central element in Aum's mission. In sermons to his disciples thereafter, Asahara spoke frequently of the need to punish humanity for its sinfulness and of how Aum would eventually have to go to war with the world at large.

These visions increased in intensity and fervor over the years, and as they did Asahara's obsessions with persecution and conspiracy grew. In the period after the 1990 election debacle, his sermons were dominated by the "conspiracy" that was seeking to destroy his movement, kill him, and eradicate the truth from this world. In this increasingly paranoid situation, Aum turned to acquiring the means with which to "defend" itself and to fight the inevitable final war. As Aum devotees worked to this end, establishing secret laboratories at Aum communes and seeking to make and procure various forms of weaponry, Asahara and his disciples became increasingly focused on the righteousness of killing. He spoke about the virtue of killing all of humanity for its sins, while his disciples displayed clear enthusiasm when he told them of their mission to do just this. By spring 1994, he had come to believe that only he could purify the world of evil, and that the time for war was nigh.[11] Within a year, the confrontation had become real, with the subway attack, the subsequent mobilization of the forces of the Japanese state against Aum, and the arrest of its leaders.

CONCLUSIONS: AUM AND THE PERILS AND
PROMISES OF RELIGION

In the above account I have focused on the earlier phases of Aum's development, because it was there that the seeds of Aum's violence were planted and developed. My analysis indicates that Aum was a religious movement, driven by a series of religious motives and meanings—*and* that it was guilty of mass murder, crimes against humanity, and crimes against its own followers. In the brief period between its foundation in 1984, and the subway attack in 1995, Aum turned from an optimistic belief in its capacity to save the world to an ultimately nihilistic position in which it believed everyone apart from a devout chosen few deserved to die. In this process it had developed an extreme sense of righteousness, enabling Aum's devotees to believe they could kill with impunity in the name of their faith, because those they killed were unworthy of living on this earth and were damned because of their bad karma. This sense of righteousness was underpinned by doctrines such as *poa* and conceptions about the rights and duties of spiritually advanced beings. Asahara, as has been noted, drew many of these ideas from other traditions, and he has been accused of deliberately searching for suitable doctrines with which to justify Aum's turn to violence. While this might be so, one should remember that Asahara did not have to look far for teachings that fitted or reinforced his world views. Buddhist notions about karma, the rights of gurus, and the flexibility of morality, for instance, enabled him to construct the doctrines of killing for salvation, while texts such as Revelation affirmed his visions of a final war and helped provide the resources through which Aum's theology of violence could coalesce into a potent and real force.

Of course one can argue that the resources Asahara drew on were meant to provide symbolic messages, that images of sacred conflict and final wars between good and evil simply indicate that the task of religions on earth is to do good and fight evil. Yet one of the basic problems (and strengths) of religious traditions and texts is their very ambiguity. They provide and are open to vastly differing explanations, and their ideas can easily be read in different ways by different people in different contexts. The same sets of religious texts—and the same traditions—can inspire multiple voices to emerge articulating multiple visions of truth. They can provide resources simultaneously for a Gandhi and a fervent Hindu nationalist, for deeply spiritual Japanese Buddhist teachers and for an Asahara, for a Rumi and a Bin Laden, for a Saint Francis and a Crusader.

One of the main lessons that can be drawn from the Aum case relates to the ambiguity of seemingly symbolic texts which can be interpreted so as to feed into, enhance, and legitimate the potential for actual violence and conflict. Promise and peril, in effect, may arise from the same sources and resources. Viewed from inside the mindset of Aum and its devotees, Aum was the supreme example of the *promise* of religion. It offered a new, better world to come, idealistic visions of the peaceful eradication of evil and the attainment of salvation, and an ideal realm on earth for all. When Aum's millennialism had become catastrophic and it believed that damnation was the fate of everyone in the material world, its devotees still believed it offered the only hope for a future in which materialism would be vanquished, the wicked would be punished, and the righteous could benefit from their spiritual endeavors. That vision was founded in a moral presumption so extreme that it provided Aum with the resources for killing. The religious views of Aum Shinrikyô gave the movement the sense of righteousness that fueled such beliefs. And they gave it the moral authority to use every means at its disposal to bring that new world about—and to fight and kill those who, the movement believed, threatened its survival and the advent of its promised realm.

In Aum the idealism that underpinned the plans to build a Lotus realm on earth and to bring about worldly salvation and the eradication of evil was transformed into a destructive philosophy in which those who sought to create that new brave world became murderers venting punishment on the unworthy. Members of Aum were convinced that even though their actions involved destruction and violence, they were right and valid, spiritual rather than criminal. As has been made clear, the violence they espoused was in itself a product of their righteousness and of their conviction that they, and they alone, possessed the truth. As such Aum Shinrikyô presents us with a potent example of how religion can give rise to peril as well as promise, and of the paradoxical situation in which people fired with spiritual beliefs that promise salvation can end up by killing the people they seek to save.

NOTES

1. For fuller details of the Aum affair see Ian Reader, *A Poisonous Cocktail? Aum Shinrikyô's Path to Violence* (Copenhagen: NIAS, 1996); idem, *Religious Violence in Contemporary Japan: The Case of Aum Shinrikyô* (Richmond, Va., and Honolulu: Curzon Press and University of Hawaii Press, 2000); and Shimazono Susumu, *Gendai shûkyô no kanôsei: Oumu Shinrikyô to bôryoku* (Tokyo: Iwanami Shoten, 1997).

2. Asahara Shôkô, *Vajrayana kôsu. Kyôgaku shisutemu kyôhon* (internal unpublished Aum document dating from c. 1994), p. 138. Hereafter referred to as Asahara VK.

3. See Robert J. Kisala and Mark R. Mullins, eds., *Religion and Social Crisis in Japan: Understanding Japanese Society through the Aum Affair* (Basingstoke, U.K., and New York: Palgrave, 2001) on the impact of the affair on Japanese society.

4. The people involved were the Japanese Shimada Hiromi and the American James R. Lewis; see my article "Scholarship, Aum Shinrikyô, and Integrity," *Nova Religio* 3, no. 2 (2000): 368–82 for further details.

5. For an extended discussion of these points see Reader, *Religious Violence in Contemporary Japan*.

6. See, for example, Donald S. Lopez, Jr., *Buddhism: An Introduction and Guide* (London and New York: Allen Lane, Penguin Press, 2001), p. 155.

7. See, for example Asahara VK (cited in note 2 above), pp. 111–12, 252.

8. Sandra Bell, "'Crazy Wisdom', Charisma, and the Transmission of Buddhism in the United States," *Nova Religio* 2, no. 1 (1998): 55–75.

9. For further discussion of these issues see Reader, *Religious Violence in Contemporary Japan*, pp. 141–43.

10. Asahara VK, pp. 31–33, in a sermon delivered on April 7, 1989, probably around one month after the killing.

11. Ibid., esp. pp. 337–38, sermons during spring 1994.

Moral Paradoxes in Hinduism
WENDY DONIGER

INTRODUCTION: PARADOX

The greatest methodological contribution that structuralism makes to our understanding of religious texts lies in Claude Lévi-Strauss's insight that every myth is driven by the obsessive need to solve a paradox *that cannot be solved,* to tidy up a mess that cannot be cleaned up.[1] In his view, myths transform the paradox into a narrative that expresses a contradiction: each myth simultaneously expresses two opposed paradigms, two human truths that are mutually opposed. (Calvin Klein's perfume called Contradiction, advertised with the slogan, "She is always and never the same," would have been called Paradox if it had been made in France.) The tension between these two paradigms holds us in suspense to the very end of the story, where we often discover that both of them are true. I am using *paradox* here in the broader sense as glossed by the Shorter Oxford English Dictionary: "statement contrary to received opinion; seemingly absurd though perhaps really well-founded statement." In this sense a paradox expresses ambivalence rather than logical self-contradiction. Thus, where Lévi-Strauss' critics see him as reducing myths to logical oppositions, I see him as illuminating human ambivalences.

In this article I will consider five paradoxes in classical Hinduism,[2] all of which put double-edged swords in the hands of religious activists and thus serve as forces for promise or peril: (1) the paradox of renunciation (and worldliness); (2) the paradox of non-injury (*ahimsa*) and eating/killing; (3) the paradox of divine sport (*lila*) and ethical action; (4) the paradox of pluralism and plenitude; and (5) the paradox of orthopraxy and heterodoxy.

106

THE PARADOX OF RENUNCIATION (AND WORLDLINESS)

The paradox of renunciation enters Indian history as a clash between triads and quartets. There are several important triads in Hinduism, and their role in Hindu intellectual history demonstrates that "three" became a kind of shorthand for "lots and lots"; these threes represented the multivalent, multifaceted, multiform, multi-whatever-you-like nature of the real phenomenal world. A basic triad was that of the three human goals (*purusharthas*, also called the triple path or *trivarga*): religious law (*dharma*), profit (*artha*), and pleasure (*kama*). For assonance, one might call them piety, profit, and pleasure; society, success, and sex; or duty, domination, and desire. Every human being—more precisely, every man (as these rules were not meant to apply to women)—was said to have a right, and even a duty, to achieve all three goals. So, too, originally, there were three stages of life (*ashramas*): study (*brahmacharya*), the householder life (*grihasthya*), and the forest-dweller stage (*vanaprastha*).[3]

But around the sixth century B.C.E., the fourth stage of the renouncer (*sannyasin*) was added to the three stages of life, forming a quartet. And at the same time, the goal of the renouncer, Freedom (*moksha*), was added to the three goals of life, so that the triple path (*trivarga*) became the quadruple path (*chaturvarga*). The Freedom proposed by this new movement was freedom from the circle of rebirth (*samsara*) and from the trap of *karma*—the actions, good and bad, that accumulate and determine one's rebirth. For from the start the idea of rebirth carries with it the idea of escaping from that circularity. To European and American thinkers, reincarnation seems to pose a possible solution to the problem of death. If you fear the cessation of life (setting aside considerations of heaven and hell), then the belief that you will, in fact, live again after you die may be of comfort: how nice to go around again and again, never to be blotted out altogether, to have more and more of life. This being so, the fact that major schools of Hindu (and Buddhist) philosophy strive to end rebirth has struck many European and American thinkers as a pessimistic or nihilistic attitude. Such Hindus (the critic reasons) are throwing away not merely the present life but all those potential future lives as well, committing a kind of serial suicide, preventative euthanasia.

But this line of reasoning entirely misses the point of the Hindu doctrine. What the authors of these early texts feared was not life but death—more precisely, "old age and death" (*jaramrityu*). And what they feared most of all was what they called "recurrent death," a series of rebirths and redeaths. As one text states, "When they die they come to life again, but they become the food of this (Death) again and again."[4] And if it is a terrible thing to grow old and die, once and for all, how much more terrible to do it over and over again? This is what the fourth goal, *moksha,* was designed to prevent.

The opposition between renunciation and worldliness was made clear when philosophers reduced the new quartet to a dualism. Freedom (*moksha* or *mukti*) came to be contrasted with the rest of the group, called "enjoyment" (*bhoksha* or *bhukti*),[5] just as asceticism was contrasted with enjoyment (*yoga* vs. *bhoga*). These dichotomies play upon the assonance between *moksha/bhoksha* and *yoga/bhoga*. People also spoke, however, of the tension between *moksha* and *dharma.* The philosophy of the Upanishads ("Vedantic philosophy") also reduced the goals of life to another dualism: what one likes (*preyas*), consisting of pleasure and profit; and what is good for one (*shreyas*), consisting of *dharma* and Freedom.[6] Moreover, the fourth goal was often, implicitly or explicitly, exalted above any of the three terms, just as the triad as a whole, as a balanced set, had originally constituted an implicit fourth term greater than any of its constituent parts.[7]

In nonrenunciatory Hinduism, each individual was supposed to follow his particular *dharma* (*svadharma*), a unique path laid out for him at birth which was primarily determined by his caste. Now the renunciatory movements proposed a single, universal *dharma* (*sanatana dharma*), involving general moral precepts such as honesty, generosity, and nonviolence.[8] This move posed a basic social paradox: if your *svadharma* was to be a warrior or a butcher, how were you to reconcile this with the universal *dharma* that imposed the strictures against taking life? We will return to this problem. Hinduism validated the diversity (and the hierarchy) of individal *dharma.* But at the same time, it validated the unity of *dharma* by endorsing *sanatana dharma.* This is the paradox of absolutism and relativism, which we know from debates within our intellectual world, too. Recently it has been seen in feminist debates about the burning of widows in India: the absolute feminist view that it is always a bad thing to encourage or allow a woman to self-immolate stands against the relativist postcolonial view that American feminists have no more business imposing their ideas upon Hindus than British imperialists had.[9]

These universalist ideas might have challenged the Vedic diversity of caste and pantheon, but instead they came to supplement them, by adding a transcendent fourth to the pre-existing material triads. The ideal of Freedom might have challenged the Vedic India of fabled elephants encrusted with jewels and temples covered with copulating couples, the world of sensuality from which the omphalosceptic yogis fled. Instead, it was reabsorbed into Vedic Hinduism and inverted into the desire to be reborn, but reborn better in worldly terms (richer, fatter, with more sons, and so forth). The triad, or the quartet, also tended to be hierarchized, and the hierarchy was envisioned differently by different people.[10] Not surprisingly, *dharma* texts tended to give *dharma* pride of place, with profit second and pleasure third. Moreover, the pervasive force of particular *dharma* extended itself over the quartet: the four goals were ranked differently according to the point of view of each individual, depending upon the person's gender, social group, and so forth. Various unsatisfactory, overlapping correlations between the four goals and the three (upper) classes were attempted: Freedom and *dharma* for Brahmins; *dharma* for Brahmins and kings; profit for kings and merchants (Vaishyas); and pleasure for kings and courtesans. But according to the Kamasutra, profit is the primary concern of both a king and a courtesan.[11] There was only a slightly better correlation with the four stages (*ashramas*): Freedom for renouncers and, with modifications, for forest-dwellers; *dharma* for forest-dwellers, students, and householders; profit and pleasure for householders. But the fit was never very good, because the two systems really express two entirely different approaches to the taxonomy of human goals.

These two basic approaches to human life, the worldly and the renunciatory, pose a conflict between the one and the many, between a unitary *dharma* and a diverse *dharma*, between renunciation and the other three stages of life. Indian tradition came up with at least five tentative solutions to this conflict.

First, it was said that the stages (or goals) were to be followed, not simultaneously, but one at a time. Freedom became a fourth stage, often indefinitely postponed while theoretically extolled. Many Hindus prayed, with Saint Augustine, "Make me chaste, O Lord, but not yet." But this trivialized the original claims of the renunciant philosophy, which were opposed to the other three stages altogether. "You are in a burning house," said the Buddha; "jump *now*." Finally, the third stage in the quartet, the forest-dweller, became highly problematic when attempts were made to distinguish it, in a temporal sequence, from the new, fourth stage.[12]

Second was the argument from symbiosis, or plentitude: the two groups need one another, to compose society as a whole. There are two forms of immortality, one achieved through one's own children and one through renunciation.[13] Thus Louis Dumont speaks of the renouncer whose holiness and knowledge are fed back into the society that supports him,[14] and Jan Heesterman speaks of the paradox of the Brahmin, who must remain outside society in order to be useful inside.[15] This is a self-contradictory situation, a Möbius strip that folds back in on itself, a metaphysical martini with a twist.

The third solution was compromise, which proved unsatisfactory for a number of reasons, but basically because compromise is not a Hindu way of solving problems.[16]

The fourth solution was identification, and it came to replace hierarchy as Vedantic thinking largely superseded Vedic thinking. Thus it was said that the householder *was* a renouncer, if he played his role correctly; that *dharma* was Freedom. As the god Krishna told prince Arjuna in the Bhagavad Gita: "Do your work [of killing your cousins] well and you win the merit of renunciation."[17] And now it was also said that one must have sons—usually regarded as the goal of the householder stage—to achieve Freedom. Tantrism (and Zen) took this line of argument to the extreme: thus, just as Freedom simply *is* enjoyment (*moksha* = *bhoksha*), so, in the formulation of the Buddhist philosopher Nagarjuna, the world of rebirth (*samsara*) simply *is* the place or condition of freedom from rebirth (*nirvana*). Four has been reduced to two and then to one. Monism has triumphed—but only in this paradigm.

The fifth, and ultimate, Hindu solution was hierarchy. Throughout classical Hindu thought, the drive to hierarchize rides roughshod over the drive to present equal alternatives or even a serial plan for a well-rounded human life.

This deep conflict built into the structure of Hinduism—the paradox of renunciation and worldliness—provides a rich menu that accommodates all religious temperaments and validates them equally. Yet it also blurs the moral imperative, saps the potential impulse for social revolution by siphoning it off into renunciation, and does not in fact value the various paths of life equally.

THE PARADOX OF NON-INJURY (*AHIMSA*) AND EATING/KILLING

When Hindus and Muslims turned on one another in violence after Partition in 1948, European and American intellectuals were astonished that the nonviolent Hindu could be violent. They were no longer so astonished in 1991, when Hindus stormed the Babri mosque in Ayodhya, which was built by the Muslim emperor Babur over the place where many Hindus believe that the god Rama was born, and over a thousand people died in subsequent riots. Daily bloodshed in India in the name of religion had become common, and people were used to the killing of Hindus by Sikhs, Sikhs by Hindus, Hindus by Muslims, Muslims by Hindus, Tamil Hindus by Buddhists, Buddhists by Tamil Hindus, Untouchables by Brahmins, Brahmins by Untouchables, and on and on.

Why did Europeans and Americans believe that Hindus were nonviolent? Is there any basis for it in the intellectual history of India? It is, I think, the intellectual rather than political history of India that has given rise to the European and American idea of Hindu nonviolence. That is, it is what Hindus have said, and what they have seemed to believe, rather than what they have done, that has led to the European and American expectation of Hindu tolerance.

The emphasis on nonviolence, *ahimsa,* that Gandhi made so famous in the West, is far from typical of Hindu thinking, let alone Hindu action. Of course, Gandhi did not invent *ahimsa;* Hindus have sworn allegiance to the concept of nonviolence at least from the time of the Laws of Manu, in the early centuries of the Common Era. "Hindu nonviolence" is certainly not an idea imposed upon Hindus by Orientalist, imperialist pressure. But it may well be that some Hindus doth protest too violently about their nonviolence; indeed, some Hindus respond violently to any slur cast against their nonviolence. This, too, is a paradox. *Ahimsa,* usually translated as "nonviolence" or "non-injury," is not merely the absence of violence. It is derived from a Sanskrit verb *han,* which means "to injure or kill," but is formed as a desiderative noun, meaning "the absence of the desire to injure or kill." It is thus a state of mind, not a policy for behavior; and, as Krishna pointed out in the Bhagavad Gita, it is quite possible to adhere to the mental principles of nonviolence while killing your cousins in battle.

Violence, like all things Indian, begins in the Rig Veda, the earliest and most revered text of the Hindu canon (composed around 1,000 B.C.E.) It is a text that reveres war; its chief god is the warrior Indra; and it revolves around the sacrifice of animals, often depicted in gruesome terms. Both the war and the sacrifice were continued and combined in the great Hindu martial epic, the Mahabharata (composed from 300 B.C.E. to 300 C.E.), which has been called a "ritual of battle." A king in this text insists: "I see no being which lives in the world without violence. Creatures exist at one another's expense; the stronger consume the weaker. The mongoose eats mice, just as the cat eats the mongoose; the dog devours the cat, O king, and wild beasts eat the dog."[18] When the violent Vedic worldview was challenged by the renunciant movements, the idea of nonviolence, that might have challenged the Vedic demand for violent sacrifice, instead came to supplement that demand, just as the ideal of Freedom supplemented the materialist triads instead of challenging them. As Frances Zimmermann points out:

> In the animal kingdom and then the human one, the dialectic of the eaten eater introduces further divisions between the strong and the weak, the predator and his prey, the carnivore and the vegetarian. Vegetarianism—a brahminic ideal and a social fact in India—precisely calls into question that fateful dialectic in which every class of being feeds on another. The prohibition of flesh, which became increasingly strict in brahminic society, was one way to break the chain of all this alimentary violence and affirm that it is not really necessary to kill in order to eat. [19]

Now, vegetarianism and nonviolence are not the same thing at all. A moment's consideration will remind us that it is usual to eat meat without killing (most European and American non-vegetarians do it every day) and equally normal to kill without eating meat (what percentage of hit men or soldiers devour their fallen enemies?). Indeed, Jan Heesterman has suggested that vegetarianism and nonviolence were originally mutually exclusive, that in the earliest period of Indian civilization, nonviolent, meat-eating householders would consecrate themselves as (violent) warriors in time of war by giving up the eating of meat.[20] They either ate meat *or* killed. In later Hinduism, the strictures against eating and killing continued to be at odds, so that it was better to kill an Untouchable than to kill a Brahmin, but better to eat a Brahmin (presuming that one came across a dead one) than to eat an Untouchable (ditto). Nevertheless, the logical assumption that any animal that one ate had to have been killed by *someone* led to a natural association between vegetarianism and nonviolence toward living creatures. And this vegetarian ideal came to prevail in India, living cheek to jowl with animal sacrifice and the practice of meat-eating.[21]

The violent Vedic worldview was both sustained and challenged by the Laws of Manu, a basic text of the dominant form of Hinduism. Probably composed sometime around the beginning of the Common Era, Manu had become the standard source of authority in the orthodox tradition within a few centuries, and has remained so. Over the course of the centuries, the text attracted nine complete commentaries, attesting to its crucial significance within the tradition. Manu's terror of anarchy, which is called the "law of the fishes," whereby bigger fish eat smaller ones in an uncontrolled universe, is a direct continuation of Vedic assumptions about natural violence, and Manu still upholds the centrality of the violent animal sacrifice that is the pivot of the Rig Veda. Thus, Manu acknowledges that "you can never get meat without violence to creatures with the breath of life, and the killing of creatures with the breath of life does not get you to heaven; therefore you should not eat meat."[22] But it also states that "killing in a sacrifice is not killing. . . . The violence to those that move and those that do not move which is sanctioned by the Veda—that is known as nonviolence."[23] By defining the sacrifice as nonviolent, Manu made it nonviolent. In this way, he was able to list the Veda and nonviolence together in his summary of the most important elements of the moral life, the basic principles of *sanatana dharma:* "The recitation of the Veda, inner heat, knowledge, the repression of the sensory powers, nonviolence, and serving the guru bring about the supreme good."[24] Later Hindus attempted to enact this uneasy resolution by using rice cakes in place of the animal victim—and "strangling" the rice cakes at the appropriate moment in the ritual.

These two basic approaches to human life, the violent and worldly, and the nonviolent and renunciatory, constitute the paradox of noninjury and killing and eating. The Vedantic reverence for nonviolence flowered in Gandhi; the Vedic reverence for violence flowered in the slaughters that followed Partition. If Gandhi hoped that the ancient Hindu ideal of nonviolence, even in its modern incarnation, would succeed in the colonial context, he was whistling in the dark—as the subsequent history of Indian independence demonstrates. Nonviolence failed because it did not pay sufficient attention to the other, more tenacious ancient Hindu ideal that had a deeper grip on real emotions in the twentieth century: violence.

At the time when Partition was being debated, a member of the Fundamentalist and anti-Muslim Hindu association (RSS) remarked that, since Hindus are known to be the least violent people in the world, they deserve to have the land of India to themselves, and therefore the (violent) Muslims should be disenfranchised:

> The spirit of broad catholicism, generosity, toleration, truth, sacrifice and love for all life, which characterizes the average Hindu mind not wholly vitiated by Western influence, bears eloquent testimony to the greatness of Hindu culture. . . . The non-Hindu peoples in Hindustan . . . must not only give up their attitude of intolerance and ungratefulness towards this land . . . but must . . . stay in the country wholly subordinated to the Hindu Nation, claiming nothing, deserving no privileges, far less any preferential treatment—not even citizen's rights.[25]

The logic of this passage admittedly reduces the argument for the disenfranchisement of Muslims to the absurd; but it expresses the extreme form of views that are held by many Hindus. And extremists are, after all, the problem; it was an RSS man who killed Gandhi. Having witnessed the carnage in Bosnia, we may also recall with particular irony that when Gandhi was asked how India was going to be able to forge a nation out of two different religious and cultural traditions, he replied, "It can be done. Look at Yugoslavia." Gandhi's over-optimistic assessment of the possibility of an enduring peace in Yugoslavia is of a piece with his over-optimistic program for India.

THE PARADOX OF DIVINE SPORT AND ETHICAL ACTION

A basic tenet of Upanishadic Hinduism is the idea that the whole universe is merely an expression of God's sport, *lila*, a kind of spectacle that he puts on for his own amusement, a play in which it is essential for each of us to determine what role is ours, and to play it.[26] *Lila* expresses all the light, aerial, frivolous, effortless, and insignificant aspects of play. Another word for play in Sanskrit is the verbal root *div*, meaning primarily "to play" but also "to shine"; in English, too, we speak both of the playing of a game and of the play of light on water.[27] Now, the Sanskrit word for "god" is *deva,* cognate with the Latin *deus,* Greek *theos,* and English "divine" and "theology." Sanskrit texts usually derive *deva,* "god," from the second meaning, "to shine," but one Sanskrit text derives it from the first: "When one speaks of the 'playing' (*divya*) of the creator, it refers to this game of his; that is why the divinities, born from that 'playing' body, are called gods (*devas*)." [28] The vision of God as a painter, dancer, storyteller, or artist pervades Hindu religious and artistic expression. It implies that life is no more real than a performance of *Hamlet,* and so you should not cry for your own father's death any more than you cry for Hamlet's death.[29]

Indeed, where Einstein reassured us that God does not play dice with the universe, Hindu theology tells us not only that He most specifically *does* play dice, but that He cheats, and is caught cheating.[30] This darker implication of God's play colors the Book of Job, where God plays a game with Satan at Job's expense, and Shakespeare's *King Lear* [4.1.36], where Gloucester remarks: "As flies to wanton boys are we to th' gods; they kill us for their sport." In his definitive study of the concept of play in human culture, Jan Huizinga refuses to pick up the religious or metaphysical aspect of *lila,* which he surely knew (since he was a Sanskritist). He writes: "Where our judgment begins to waver, the feeling that the world is serious after all wavers with it. Instead of the old saw: 'All is vanity,' the more positive conclusion forces itself upon us that 'all is play'. A cheap metaphor, no doubt, mere impotence of the mind."[31]

The problem is that the idea of the illusory nature of the world smacks of fascism. It recalls the ethical problems raised by the idea of the Nietzschean Superman, later the Nazi superman: Once the Superman realizes that nothing matters, that all is a game, he can watch other people play by the rules while he himself remains on the sidelines and does whatever he wants. And, in fact, the "it is all a game" philosophy of the Upanishads was appropriated in the Bhagavad Gita to justify war: you may kill, indeed *must* kill, for neither the killer nor the victim is real. This Hindu view appealed greatly to Nietzsche; but it is a dangerous game.[32] The Hindus themselves have always recognized that *lila* is a metaphysical image but not a guide for ethical action; we are not to imitate God; *quod licet jovi non licet bovi* ("What is permitted to Jove is not permitted to a bull"). God is playful, but, except for carnival moments like Holi, we may not play as he does. Both the Laws of Manu and the Indian philosophical texts provide a metaphysical frame for the rest of the text, which often includes a most detailed and explicit ethics. Yet the metaphysics often implies a different ethics, and we might ask if there cannot be an ethics of play, or, rather, if the moral and the aesthetic are necessarily so disjoint.[33] This philosophical richness conceals deep ethical shoals. It expresses the paradox of divine sport and ethical action.

THE PARADOX OF PLURALISM AND PLENITUDE

The paradox of the worldly and the renunciatory was easily assimilated to the paradox of the pluralistic and the monistic. For though monism remained alive and well in India, in other parts of the forest, pluralism continued to obey the command to be fruitful and multiply. Against the ancient triads, or against the whole pluralist vision, monism raised its ugly head. The renunciatory philosophies of the Upanishads (as well as of Buddhism, Jainism, and other sects) were both intellectually and sociologically monistic. Intellectually, these new religious movements envisioned a single godhead—alongside, underneath, within the apparent polytheistic pantheon.

Max Müller coined a term to describe the pluralism of the Rig Veda: kathenotheism or henotheism. It is a theological parallel to serial monogamy—the worship of a number of gods, one at a time, regarding each as the supreme, or even the only, god while you are talking to him: "You [Susan, Vishnu] are the only woman/god I've ever loved; you are the only one." "You [Helen, Varuna] are the only woman/god I've ever loved; you are the only one." This made a kind of nonhierarchical pantheon possible; the attitude to each god was hierarchical ("You are the best"), but the various competing monisms cancelled one another out, so that the total picture was one of equality: each of several was the best. Hinduism is intellectually pluralistic in a manner reminiscent of the Rig Veda's kathenotheism: in Hinduism, each sect theoretically acknowledges the existence of gods other than their god(s), agrees that they are suitable for others to worship, but does not itself care to worship them. On the other hand, when it comes to sociological pluralism, there is a further split: the doctrine of *varnashramadharma* sees all social roles as equally valid from the God's-eye view, and regards the world of action as cumulatively pluralistic, exemplifying a desirable plenitude. Ultimately, this plenitude extends to a proposed solution to the problem of evil: cancer and moral evil must exist, to make the universe complete. But it gives the *individual* no choice at all in his or her social role, no pluralism of action, though the hierarchy of values assigned to different roles might well have inspired the wish to make such choices. For, as with the pigs in Orwell's *Animal Farm,* it appears that though all social roles are equal (in the eyes of God), some are more equal than others (in the eyes of men and women). This is the paradox of sociological pluralism.

Plenitude, in Hinduism, encompasses the basic concept that you can never dispose of evil but must accept it as an inevitable shadow of the good. Even the Kamasutra uses this logic. When pragmatists argue that *kama* should be avoided, because many people have been destroyed by desire, the author of the Kamasutra replies that pleasures such as sex are a means of sustaining the body, just like food, but that people must be aware of the flaws in pleasures, flaws that are like diseases.[34] The commentator explains, "People must be aware in order to take preventive measures, just as they take measures against the diseases of the body such as indigestion." Good always brings in its train the essential threat of evil. At best, you can move the inevitable evil to some other place where it does not do *you* any harm. Throughout the Puranas, the medieval Sanskrit compendia of Hinduism, we encounter myths in which a fire so intense that it threatens to destroy the universe is contained, temporarily, until the time for doomsday will come. Often this doomsday *in nuce* is said to reside in the mouth of a mare, held in hair-trigger check by the floods at the bottom of the ocean, until she is given the signal to burst out at doomsday.[35] So, too, the great cobra Kaliya kept gobbling up the little boys who went swimming in his part of the river until the child Krishna danced on his many heads and trampled him into submission; the wives of Kaliya pleaded for mercy, not wanting to become widows, and Krishna refrained from killing Kaliya but merely transported him to a certain pool, far outside the village.[36]

There is a Sanskrit saying that some problems are solved only "in the manner of the king's men" [*rajapurushanyayat*]: you call in the soldiers to get rid of the dacoits, and they do, but then the soldiers remain in your village, and wreak worse mayhem than the dacoits had done. Demons often pose this problem. You create a terrible goddess to kill the demon, and she does, but then you have to deal with the goddess. Many Sanskrit myths composed in the north of India dispose of their cosmological garbage by sending the offending creature south, over the Vindhya mountains, into the southern territory that northern Brahmins regarded as beyond the pale. (In the Hollywood mythology of the 1950s, creatures from outer space usually came from, or returned to, Mexico in this way; in British movies, it was Wales.) This mythology suggests that the theory of plenitude actually functions as a theory of limited good in another guise: evil must exist, but not for us, if possible; let someone else have it. The human implications of such a mythology are clear enough; it can lead to a vicious communalism. This is the paradox of plenitude.

THE PARADOX OF ORTHOPRAXY AND HETERODOXY

The pluralistic world of Vedic and Puranic ritual is primarily orthoprax but heterodox. That is, it does not insist on doctrine (*doxis*) as long as ritual and social behavior (*praxis*) satisfies the standards of the particular group (usually a small caste group). By contrast, the monistic world, that is, the world of philosophy, is primarily orthodox. Renunciant sects, which are monistic both sociologically and intellectually, often flaunt outlandishly antisocial behavior (going naked, eating out of human skulls, and so forth). But they believe that there is only one correct belief.

In the course of Indian history, the monistic view turned itself inside out to generate yet another sort of tolerance. It argued not only that all physical and immaterial things were one, but that all *religions* were also one, that Muslims and Christians really worshipped the same god that Hindus worshipped, but just called him Allah or Christ. (This led to interesting misunderstandings when Christian missionaries fired their cannons across the bows of South Asians.) The Mughal Emperor Akbar, for instance, was a true pluralist; born a Muslim but with a Hindu wife, he entertained a veritable circus of holy men at his multireligious salons. He flirted with Christianity to such a degree that the missionaries congratulated themselves that he was on the brink of converting—until they realized that he still continued to worship at mosques, and, indeed, Hindu temples. An inscription for a Temple in Kashmir, composed by Abu al-Fazl ibn Mubarak (1551–1602), Akbar's minister and chronicler, reads:

O God, in every temple I see people that see thee, and in every language I hear spoken, people praise thee. Polytheism and Islam feel after thee. Each religion says, "Thou art one, without equal." If it be a mosque people murmur the holy prayer, and if it be a Christian Church, people ring the bell from love to Thee. Sometimes I frequent the Christian cloister, and sometimes the mosque. But it is thou whom I search from temple to temple. Thy elect have no dealings with either heresy or orthodoxy; for neither of them stands behind the screen of thy truth. Heresy to the heretic, and religion to the orthodox, but the dust of the rose petal belongs to the heart of the perfume seller.[37]

This (surely rather loose) English translation of the inscription inspired Alfred Lord Tennyson to write a poem entitled "Akbar's Dream."[38] The poem is long, but my favorite passage is this one, a statement by Akbar to Abul Fazl (as Abu al-Fazl was generally known in English):

> Sit by my side. While thou art one with me,
> I seem no longer like a lonely man
> In the king's garden, gathering here and there
> From each fair plant the blossom choicest-grown
> To wreathe a crown not only for the king
> But in due time for every Mussulman,
> Brahmin, and Buddhist, Christian, and Parsee,
> Thro' all the warring world of Hindustan.
> Well spake thy brother in his hymn to heaven
> "Thy glory baffles wisdom. All the tracks
> Of science making toward Thy Perfectness
> Are blinding desert sand; we scarce can spell
> The Alif of Thine alphabet of Love."

Later in the poem he speaks of wanting to "beat back / The menacing poison of intolerant priests, Those cobras ever setting up their hoods." Then he tells Abul Fazl his dream:

> Well, I dream'd
> That stone by stone I rear'd a sacred fane,
> A temple, neither Pagod, Mosque, nor Church,
> But loftier, simpler, always open-door'd.
> To every breath from heaven, and Truth and Peace
> And Love and Justice came and dwelt therein.

> But while we stood rejoicing, I and thou,
> I heard a mocking laugh "the new Koran!"
> And on the sudden, and with a cry "Saleem"
> Thou, thou—I saw thee fall before me, and then
> Me too the black-wing'd Azrael overcame.
> But death had ears and eyes; I watch'd my son,
> And those that follow'd, loosen stone from stone,
> All my fair work; and from the ruin arose
> The shriek and curse of trampled millions, even
> As in the time before; but while I groan'd,
> From out the sunset pour'd an alien race,
> Who fitted stone to stone again, and Truth,
> Peace, Love and Justice came and dwelt therein.
> Nor in the field without were seen or heard
> Fires of Suttee, nor wail of baby-wife,
> Or Indian widow; and in sleep I said
> "All praise to Allah by whatever hands
> My mission be accomplish'd!" but we hear
> Music: our palace is awake, and morn
> Has lifted the dark eyelash of the Night
> From off the rosy cheek of waking Day.
> Our hymn to the sun. They sing it. Let us go.

Tennyson still cannot resist an intolerant slur against "the warring world" of Hinduism (suttee, the mistreatment of widows, child brides, and all that), but the poem ends with a hymn to the sun which is Hindu in its inspiration, even if it is thoroughly Anglican in its execution. For after the "son" of Akbar has undone all his good works (it was actually Akbar's grandson, Aurungzeb), the "alien race" that will pour "from out the sunset" (that is, the West) to rebuild the shattered pluralistic dream is, of course, the British.

Logically, the sort of universalism that argues that "in every temple I see people that see thee" should have led polytheistic Hindus to the belief that there was no point in trying to convert a Muslim to Hinduism. This was, however, not always the case. Vedic, orthoprax Hindus certainly made no efforts to convert anyone to Hinduism, arguing that you had to be born a Hindu to be a Hindu. But Vedantic, heteroprax Hindus in the shadows of orthodoxy argued that *their* particular brand of monism was more monistic than thou. Thus, unlike orthoprax Hindus, these sects have often proselytized. It might well be argued that this sort of conversion is a form of intellectual violence commensurate with the physical violence of enforced behavior. For, although proselytizing is not in itself necessarily intolerant, it does close the open-ended door of pluralism. Thus, Krishna in the Bhagavad Gita allows that all other gods are aspects of himself, but still suggests that the best, quickest, most secure way to God is directly through him: "When their wits are stolen away by their desires, people seek other gods . . . but whatever body a devotee wishes to honor with faith, I confirm that faith in him, making it unwavering. But the reward of those men of small minds is limited. Those who sacrifice to the gods go to the gods, but those who are devoted to me and sacrifice to me go to me."[39] And: "Even those who are devoted to other gods and sacrifice to them, filled with faith, they too really sacrifice to me. For I am the one who enjoys all sacrifices, but they do not recognize me truly, and so they fall away."[40]

Medieval, Puranic Hinduism (which is alive and well in many parts of India today) is a strange mixture of these two currents that join but never merge, like streams of oil and water. Ritually, Puranic Hindus are orthoprax. The fanatics among them kill people (such as Muslims) who *act* wrongly, for example, by not respecting the bounds of the caste system, while the majority, philosophically heterodox, view with respectful or disdainful tolerance the divergent views of other religions. There is a long legacy of this tolerance, going back to the Muslim-Hindu saint Kabir and the whole Sant tradition, who fought and fight against identity politics. And there is growing contemporary evidence that many Hindus and Muslims continue to live together in harmony in the teeth of prevailing political madness.[41] Some Hindus within the traditional, Puranic fold, however, are philosophically Vedantic, orthodox, and correspondingly intolerant of deviant doctrines. This gives them yet another reason, exacerbating their orthoprax reasons, to try to convert (or even kill) people like Muslims. This is the paradox of orthopraxy and heterodoxy.

CONCLUSION

These deep structures of paradox in Hinduism lead to a number of moral quandaries, some of which Hinduism is well equipped to address, through its doctrines of renunciation, non-injury, divine sport, pluralism, plenitude, and orthopraxy. But as we have seen, these same doctrines are themselves (to lapse into the hippy diction of the 1960s), if not part of the solution, part of the problem. That is the paradox.

NOTES

1. Claude Lévi-Strauss, "The Structural Study of Myth," in *Structural Anthropology,* trans. Claire Jacobson and Brooke Grundfest Schoepf (Harmondsworth: Penguin Books, 1963), pp. 206–31; and "The Story of Asdiwal," in *The Structural Study of Myth and Totemism,* ed. Edmund Leach (London: Tavistock Publications, 1967), pp. 27–30.

2. This article was first presented as a lecture at Boston University on April 3, 2002. David Eckel's wise and learned response at that time provided much food for thought, some of which has found its way into this revised version of that talk.

3. See *The Laws of Manu,* trans. Wendy Doniger with Brian K. Smith (Harmondsworth: Penguin Books, 1991), 6.87–94 for the stages of life.

4. *Shatapatha Brahmana* (Benares: Chowkhamba Sanskrit Series, 1964), 10.4.4.1–3. Cited in Wendy Doniger O'Flaherty, *The Origins of Evil in Hindu Mythology* (Berkeley: University of California Press, 1976), p. 217.

5. From the verb *bhuj,* which means a whole group of delicious things: the enjoyment or consumption of food, sex, experience, *karma,* or fuel (by fire).

6. Charles Malamoud, "Sémantique et rhétorique dans la hiérarchie hindoue des 'buts de l'homme,'" in *Cuir le monde: Rite et pensée dans l'inde ancienne* (Paris: éditions la Découverte, 1989), p. 142.

7. Ibid., p. 146.

8. For the tension between *svadharma* (particular *dharma*) and *sanatana dharma* (general *dharma*), see the stories of the two demons, Harikesha and Sukeshin, in Doniger O'Flaherty, *Origins of Evil in Hindu Mythology,* pp. 94–97 and 128–31.

9. See Wendy Doniger, "Why Did They Burn?" A review of three books about widow burning by Lata Mani, Catherine Weinberger-Thomas, and Mala Sen, *Times Literary Supplement,* 14 September 2001, pp. 3–4.

10. See Friedrich Wilhelm in *The Concept of Duty in South Asia,* ed. Wendy Doniger O'Flaherty and J. Duncan Derrett (London: School of Oriental and African Studies; Delhi: Vikas Publishing Company; Columbia, Mo.: South Asia Books, 1978).

11. *The Kamasutra of Vatsyayana,* a new translation with introduction and commentary by Wendy Doniger with Sudhir Kakar (London and New York: Oxford World Classics, 2002), 1.2.15.

12. See Wendy Doniger O'Flaherty, *Siva: The Erotic Ascetic* (London and Oxford: Oxford University Press, 1973).

13. Ibid., pp. 76–77.

14. Louis Dumont, *Homo Hierarchicus* (Paris, 1967); *Homo Hierarchicus: The Caste System and Its Implications,* trans. Mark Saisbury, Louis Dumont, and Basia Gulati (Chicago: University of Chicago Press, 1980).

15. J. C. Heesterman, *The Inner Conflict of Society: Essays in Indian Ritual, Kingship, and Society* (Chicago: University of Chicago Press, 1985).

16. See Doniger O'Flaherty, *Siva,* for a discussion of myths of forest-dwellers.

17. *Bhagavad Gita: Mahabharata* (Poona: Bhandarkar Oriental Research Institute, 1933–69), 6.23–40.

18. *Mahabharata* (Southern Recension) 12.15.10ff., trans. David Shulman, *The King and the Clown in South Indian Myth and Poetry* (Princeton, N.J.: Princeton University Press, 1985), p. 29.

19. Frances Zimmermann, *The Jungle and the Aroma of Meats* (Berkeley: University of California Press, 1987), pp. 1–2.

20. Jan Heesterman, *The Inner Conflict of Tradition* (Chicago: University of Chicago Press, 1985).

21. For a discussion of the synthesis of sacrificial and antisacrificial traditions in India, and the parallel developments in Judaism and Christianity, see Wendy Doniger O'Flaherty, *Other Peoples' Myths: The Cave of Echoes* (New York: Macmillan; London: Collier Macmillan, 1988), chap. 4.

22. *Laws of Manu* 5.48.

23. Ibid., 5.39, 44.

24. Ibid., 12.83–93. For other lists of standard virtues, see 6.91–94 and 10.64.

25. M. S. Golwalkar, *We or Our Nationhood Defined* (Nagpur: Bharat Prakashan, 1947), pp. 48–49 and 55–56.

26. David Haberman, *Acting as a Means of Salvation* (New York: Oxford University Press, 1988).

27. Indeed, according to the *Oxford English Dictionary,* this meaning, of the "play of light or colour," is one of the most basic, the second (after "exercise, brisk or free movement") of over thirty definitions. Then comes "sexual indulgence (now obsolete)," "jest, fun, sport," then "play of words." From 1300, "a crafty or underhanded act, a trick, dodge, or game," and "a device of magic."

28. *Brahmanda Purana* (Bombay: Venkateshvara Steam Press, 1857), 1.2.8.1–61.

29. Indeed, this is the very advice that Hamlet's mother gives him, and that he of course ignores: do not privilege the particular (*svadharma*) over the common (*sanatana dharma*).

30. Wendy Doniger, *The Bedtrick: Tales of Sex and Masquerade* (Chicago: University of Chicago Press, 2000); David Shulman and Don Handelman, *God Inside Out: Siva's Game of Dice* (New York: Oxford University Press, 1997).

31. Johan Huizinga, *Homo Ludens: A Study of the Play Element in Culture* (Boston: Beacon Press, 1955).

32. *Brahmanda Purana* 1.2.8.1–61.

33. I am indebted for this insight to Lorraine Daston, personal communication, 22 November 2001.

34. *Kamasutra* 1.2.32, 34, 37–38.

35. Doniger O'Flaherty, *Siva*.

36. *Bhagavata Purana* 10.15–17; trans. Wendy Doniger O'Flaherty (Harmondsworth: Penguin Books, 1975), pp. 221–28.

37. *The A'in-i Akbari [by] Abu'l-Fazl 'Allami*, trans. H. Blochmann, ed. S. L. Goomer (1871; reprint ed., Delhi: Aadiesh Book Depot, 1965), p. xxxii.

38. Alfred Lord Tennyson, "Akbar's Dream," in *Demeter and Other Poems* (vol. 7 of the *Works*) (London: Macmillan, 1908), pp. 139–48. I am indebted to Eric Ziolkowski for telling me about this poem and supplying me with a copy of it.

39. *Bhagavad Gita* 7.20–23.

40. Ibid., 79.23–25.

41. Peter Gottschalk, *Beyond Hindu and Muslim: Multiple Identity in Narratives from Rural India* (Oxford: Oxford University Press, 2001).

Author Index

Subject Index